GEOFF HURST,

THE HAND OF GOD

AND THE

BIGGEST
ROWS

IN WORLD

FOOTBALL

Also by Graham Poll

Seeing Red

Graham Poll

GEOFF HURST,
THE HAND OF GOD
AND THE
BIGGEST
ROWS
IN WORLD
FOOTBALL

HarperSport
An Imprint of HarperCollins*Publishers*

HarperSport
an imprint of HarperCollins
77–85 Fulham Palace Road,
Hammersmith, London W6 8JB

www.harpercollins.co.uk

First published in 2009

10 9 8 7 6 5 4 3 2 1

© Graham Poll 2009

Graham Poll asserts the m̶oral right to be
identified as the author of t̶h̶i̶s̶ ̶w̶o̶r̶k̶

A catalogue record of this b̶ook is
available from the British L̶ibrary

ISBN 978-0-00-731374-7

Printed and bound in Great Britain by
Clays Ltd, St Ives plc

Mixed Sources
Product group from well-managed
forests and other controlled sources
www.fsc.org Cert no. SW-COC-1806
© 1996 Forest Stewardship Council

FSC is a non-profit international organisation established to promote the
responsible management of the world's forests. Products carrying the FSC
label are independently certified to assure consumers that they come
from forests that are managed to meet the social, economic and
ecological needs of present and future generations.

Find out more about HarperCollins and the environment at
www.harpercollins.co.uk/green

CONTENTS

DEDICATION

I appreciate and thank Julia, Gemma, Josie and Harry for their support but dedicate this book to the man who introduced me to football, refereeing and life – Henry James Poll, aka 'Big Jim', aka my dad.

INTRODUCTION

On 22 June 2006, in the World Cup in Germany, I showed the yellow card to an Australian-born player twice but did not send him off.

On 22 June 1974, in the World Cup in Germany, another referee showed his yellow card twice to an Australian player and did not realize. It was the same mistake, in astonishingly similar circumstances, precisely 32 years earlier – but what happened next was very different.

In my match, Australia versus Croatia in Stuttgart, I showed Josep Simunic two yellows but later sent him off, belatedly, after brandishing a third yellow at him. Hardly a day goes by, still, without my having to hear people making what they think is a joke about it.

In the 1974 game, Australia versus Chile in Berlin, the referee was Jafar Namdar, from Iran. He cautioned Australia's Ray Richards in the first half and then, six minutes from the end of the game, booked Richards again for time-wasting. Namdar did not get his red card out. Instead, he trotted away, unaware he had now cautioned Richards twice.

Up in the stand, the Welsh referee Clive Thomas was watching. He realized the mistake and made it his business to find a FIFA official to point out what had happened. The official hurriedly told another FIFA man, who dashed down to the side of the pitch and informed the nearest linesman. Cue some frantic flag waving. Eventually, although four minutes had passed since referee Namdar had shown the second yellow card to Richards, he showed him the red.

If only someone – anyone! – had got the message to me 32 years later. If only someone had written a book about World Cup controversies after 1974; perhaps I would have read it, learned, and lived happily every after.

Now I have written that book. I have looked at ten major controversial incidents from different World Cups. I have examined them from a modern perspective, compared them with very recent controversies in the Premier League, and discovered how the game has changed, how refereeing has changed – and how some things have not altered at all.

But this is not a refereeing book. It is a football book, because I am passionate about the game and I hope that this book will enable anyone who shares that passion to notice more of what goes on during games. I hope it helps interpret events with a deeper perception. For example, did petty rivalry between the match officials help Diego Maradona get away with the 'Hand of God' goal he punched in against England? And why, when I was refereeing, did I sometimes deliberately give a foul for one team or find a reason to book a player from the other team?

I'll clear up those and many other mysteries and explode some of the myths of the game as well. Then, the next time the bloke behind you at a match shouts, 'You don't know what you're doing,' at a ref, you'll be informed enough to decide whether the spectator is correct!

So that is what this book is. Now let me tell you what it is not. It is not me saying, 'I wouldn't have done that,' or, 'I would have done it this way.' After all, who am I to sit in judgement on World Cup referees after what happened to me? But writing this book, and really scrutinizing all the incidents, ancient and modern, has been a learning process for me. I hope reading it is stimulating for you. Anyone interested in football can gain knowledge from looking at its major controversies. By increasing our understanding, we can all enhance our enjoyment of football.

GEOFF HURST,

THE HAND OF GOD

AND THE

BIGGEST
ROWS

IN WORLD

FOOTBALL

1

REPUTATIONS ON THE LINE

THE MATCH

On the one occasion England won the World Cup, the Final swung in our favour because the match officials gave a goal when the ball did not cross the line. I would like to think that now, more than forty years on, the officials would get it right if a similar incident occurred. Yet the thing that scares me is that they might not. The 2010 World Cup Final could be determined by a 'goal' that is not a goal, and this time it might be England who lose out.

By stating that modern referees and assistants ought to get it correct, I am not saying that makes me, or any of the current refs, better than the man in charge that day in 1966, Gottfried Dienst. I am not saying that at all. I can understand how and why, in the circumstances of the time, the goal was allowed. But the world has changed and so has refereeing.

It would have been a bit difficult for me to ref the 1966 Final, because it was the day after my third birthday. It was before some of you were born, no doubt. But football folk know that one of England's goals was among the most dubious ever allowed in a major match.

So let's go back to the sunny afternoon of 30 July 1966. Wembley was full but the country's streets were empty. The nation was watching black and white TV coverage of the World Cup Final. An astonishing drama unfolded.

Helmut Haller shot West Germany into the lead after twelve minutes but, seven minutes later, Geoff Hurst headed an equalizer. Then, deep into the second half, Martin Peters scored. It was 2–1 to England. We thought we'd won. But, as the very last seconds ebbed away, the Germans were given a free-kick. George Cohen blocked it but the ball bobbled across the six-yard box ... and Wolfgang Webber dived in, feet first, to score. It was 2–2. Extra-time.

Alf Ramsey, the England manager, told his troops, 'You have won the World Cup once. Now go and win it again', and eleven minutes into the extra period, Alan Ball galloped down the right and slung in a low cross. It went behind Hurst, who had to stop and turn around, so he had his back to goal when the ball reached him. He controlled it with the inside of his right foot, swivelled around, took a couple of staccato steps and slammed in a shot against the bar. The ball ricocheted down ...

On BBC television, Kenneth Wolstenholme described the tense events. 'Ball, running himself flat. Now Hurst. Can he do it? He has done! Yes! Yes. NO! No. The linesman says No.' There was a long pause. Then Wolstenholme repeated, in a deflated tone, 'The linesman says No.'

The little referee, Herr Dienst, bustled over to the much taller linesman, Tofik Bakhramov. No more than three or four words were exchanged. Abruptly, the referee turned towards the halfway line, put his whistle to his mouth and blew. Wolstenholme screamed, 'It's a goal! It's a goal!' His ecstatic response must have been matched in front rooms and parlours all over England.

The goal was awarded, and it turned the tide of the match emphatically and decisively in England's favour. Just before the end of the second period of extra-time, as Hurst loped up field one more time, there was some more memorable commentary. Wolstenholme ad-libbed the lines that have become immortal. 'Some people are on the pitch. They think it's all over. It is now!' Hurst had drilled another shot into the German net. It was 4–2. England were champions of the planet.

THE ISSUES

When we consider the controversy over Hurst's crucial second goal, the remarkable thing is that there wasn't any. There was no dissent at all at the time. Hurst, who was eventually knighted for his heroics, will tell you that not a single day has passed since 30 July 1966 without someone debating whether the ball crossed the line. But there was no argument during the game. Watching the footage again, the most astounding aspect (apart from the fact that the linesman had a belt and a substantial belly!) was how genteel it all was. Our chaps did not harangue the ref to give the goal. When he did, there was not even a whimper from the Germans.

In the modern game, players have tantrums if throw-in decisions go against them. If the events of 1966 were repeated now, there would be riots. Yet only Webber of Germany and our Roger Hunt ambled over as the referee went to talk to the linesman. Neither player said anything. Once the decision had been made, Webber reached out briefly (as if about to tap the ref on his shoulder from behind and say something), thought better of it, withdrew his arm, meekly jogged into position and readied himself for the restart.

While I was writing this book, I was at a lunch and found myself sitting next to Roger Hunt. I asked him two questions. The first was, 'Why didn't you bang the ball in to make sure when it bounced down from the bar?' People have always pointed to the fact that he did not do so as evidence that he must have believed the ball had already crossed the line. But he said that he couldn't have got to it in time. A defender nipped in and headed the ball away over the bar. My second question was, 'Why didn't the England players and the West Germans crowd around the ref and the linesman?'

He replied, 'We wouldn't have dreamed of doing that. It wouldn't have occurred to us to do that. The referee said it was a goal, so it was a goal.'

There were far fewer TV cameras and, remember, no replays. When something happened during a match, you saw it from one angle at normal speed and nobody was able to review it. So nobody was sure whether the ball had crossed the goal-line or not. Nobody saw the incident again after it had happened – not Wolstenholme, nor any of the media, nor anyone sitting at home. They were forced to rely on an independent arbiter – the linesman – and accept his ruling.

Admittedly, it was not always peace and tranquillity, even in those days. In England's 1966 quarter-final, Argentina's captain, Antonio

Rattin, was sent off but refused to leave the pitch for several minutes. Yet mostly, when there was uncertainty about events, players were much more prepared to take the word of the neutral judges – the match officials. Times change. But the role of the referee and assistants has not. They are still merely independent arbiters. It is the attitude towards them that has changed.

That said, it wasn't a goal! When I talked to Roger Hunt at that lunch in December 2008 he was still unequivocal in his belief that it was, that the ball did cross the line. But the Germans never thought it was a goal, and the day after the Final some newspaper photographs appeared to show the ball bouncing on the line and not over it. Those pictures cast the first shadows of real doubt in this country. Then, months later, a film of the 1966 World Cup was released. It was called *Goal!* but showed more clearly that it wasn't a goal. The film included the first slowed-down footage of the ball bouncing down from the crossbar. Since then, as film and television technology has developed, it has become possible to look at the incident frame by frame. Computer simulations of the moment have been created. It wasn't a goal. It was such an injustice, in fact, that the expression '*Wembley tor*' has entered the German vernacular. It is used to describe anything undeserved.

The more you look at it, the more difficult it becomes to work out why the linesman convinced himself that the ball had completely crossed the line. It was a brave decision by Tofik Bakhramov, but it was wrong, and a major factor was probably that he was not a specialist linesman. Before 1994, only referees went to World Cups. No linesmen went, so the refs took turns at running the lines. Bakhramov was the top ref in Azerbaijan and would not have operated regularly as a linesman for many years. These days a specialist 'assistant referee' would get the job. I know, to my cost, that they can make mistakes as well, but they are much less likely to do so than someone who usually referees and then suddenly has to use the different set of skills needed on the line. We'll have a look at the linesman's job in Chapter Two, when we deal with the 2006 World Cup Final and Zinedine Zidane's sending off. But for now, let's just agree that being a linesman is something that needs practice – and that Bakhramov was out of practice.

Another difficulty was that the match officials did not share a common language. It was a problem that was apparent throughout the tournament. Jack Taylor, who refereed the 1974 Final, also officiated in 1966 and said, 'With the shortage of interpreters, referees at early matches [in the 1966 finals] were often unable to give their linesmen proper instructions before going out.'

At the Final, referee Dienst was Swiss and spoke German, some French and a little English. Bakhramov was from Azerbaijan. Because his country was then in the Soviet Union, he became known after 1966 as 'the Russian linesman' but he was not Russian and only spoke a few words of Russian. He spoke Azerbaijani.

So consider that prolonged period, after England's controversial third goal, when commentator Kenneth Wolstenholme believed the linesman had said 'No'.

Did Bakhramov initially indicate No and then change his mind? Or was there confusion about what he had signalled? What was said in the very brief conversation between the ref and linesman? Did they really converse at all, if they could not speak a common language?

The joke in refereeing circles is that dear old Bakhramov was like those folk you sometimes meet on your travels abroad. You ask, 'Do you speak English?' They nod and say, 'Ye-es'. You ask, 'Which is the way to the station?' They nod and say, 'Ye-es'.

Is it possible that, whatever Dienst had said, Bakhramov would have nodded and said, 'Ye-es'? Probably not. But it is certainly true that if referees and their assistants do not have a common language then problems can develop. So, since the early 1990s, FIFA, the game's world governing body, have insisted that all officials at major tournaments speak one language – English. They have to sit English exams. So, although there is an adage about football being a universal language, nowadays the universal language of football is English.

In 1994, FIFA started using a referee and one linesman from the same country in tournament matches. The other linesman was supposed to be someone who spoke their language well. So, for instance, in that year Philip Don, who went on to become my boss as the first manager of the Select Group of professional referees in England, was selected for the World Cup in the United States and Roy Pearson, a miner's son from Durham, went with him as 'his' linesman. It was hoped that the other linesman in their matches would be someone from an English-speaking nation – Canada or Malta, for instance. Yet, in fact, in the two matches Philip was given in the World Cup he had a Finnish linesman in one and a Korean in the other.

By the time the European Championships of 2000 came around, they had sorted that out a bit better and so, when I reffed in that tournament, my assistants were Phil Sharp, from Hertfordshire, and Eddie Foley from the Republic of Ireland. Then, four years later, came the next, logical development. It was decided that, from 2004, every match in major tournaments would have a team of three officials from the same country – a ref and two assistants. In theory that ensures there are no communication difficulties at all.

Now let me tell you more about modern refereeing – and why 21st-century officials probably would not have allowed Hurst's goal. Let me start with what refs tell their assistants.

Referees, assessors and all reasonable people (so not some TV pundits or certain managers) understand that assistants can't see everything. Players can obstruct the view, or the assistant might be looking at another area of the field, or have a bad angle. That's understandable. That's acceptable. The biggest mistake an assistant can make is to think he has seen something that has not actually happened. Referees don't want assistants guessing, or reacting to instinct. We want them telling us what they have definitely, clearly seen. So, although all referees have different set speeches, I guarantee that one theme is common in pre-match instructions. The ref will tell his assistants, 'I'll forgive you if something happens and you don't see it, but I don't want you to "see" something that doesn't happen.'

Remember – and this applies to referees as well as assistants – if you do not signal for an offence, it does not mean you are saying it did not happen. It just means you didn't see it. Signalling for an offence indicates that you are certain you saw it. So the key instruction to assistants boils down to this: do not give a decision if there is any doubt in your mind. If that instruction had been given in 1966, our friend Tofik Bakhramov should surely not have given the goal. He must have had doubts.

Something else has changed since 1966 and it has fundamentally altered the way refs and assistants work. At the top of the modern game, match officials wear microphones and ear-pieces to talk to each other. They were introduced first in the English Premiership in time for the 1999/2000 season. Initially, we used to get interference from taxi firms, pizza delivery companies and so on. When you were trying to find out why your assistant had flagged for a foul by Roy Keane at Old Trafford, you would hear crackling instructions for the delivery of a thin-crust pepperoni!

But the equipment got better and, eventually, became extremely reliable. The microphones are kept 'open', which means that if either assistant says something, the ref can hear it clearly, and vice versa. So, in my 33 Premier League games in my final season for instance (2006/07), there was no real need for me to go over to an assistant. I could just talk to him via my microphone.

So why is it that, occasionally, a referee does walk over and talk to his assistant? Well, in my case, there were two sets of circumstances when, despite having radio contact, I would go to an assistant. The first was to send a message to the players, crowd, the media and TV audience. By going over to the assistant I was saying, 'This is a big decision and we are consulting. This is not something we are doing without due consideration.' I was demonstrating to everyone that the officials were in agreement.

The second circumstance in which I would go over to an assistant would be if a major decision was involved and I was not convinced the assistant had got it right. On those occasions, I wanted to look into his eyes and gauge whether he was calm and sure or panicky and unsure.

So, let me put myself in the boots of Herr Dienst and imagine that the radio communications system had been in use in 1966. As soon as Hurst's shot bounced down from the crossbar, I would have said into my lip microphone, 'Was that in?' Perhaps Bakhramov's response would have been to prevaricate or to admit that he was slightly unsure. That would have been enough to persuade me not to give the goal. Then I would have gone over to him, talking all the time, saying things like, 'If we have any doubt, we must not give it. The world will understand if we get it wrong in those circumstances. But if it did not cross the line and we say it did, we are in trouble.' If it had been me, then when I had got there I would have looked into his eyes. I would have said something like, 'We know the importance of this decision, so are you absolutely sure the ball crossed the line completely?' If there was a shred of doubt in the linesman's mind, he should have shaken his head and we should have restarted play with a corner (because, after Hurst's shot had bounced down, a German defender headed the ball out of play over the bar).

There is someone else I'd have asked for help in my era but Herr Dienst didn't have: the Fourth Official. It was in 1991 that Fourth Officials were introduced and sent to games to act as back-up. They also wear microphones and ear-pieces. Their duties include intervening in certain specified circumstances to inform the ref about events on the field. But the Fourth Official is not supposed to tell the ref about things he has spotted on a TV screen which happens to be near him. That's the theory. In practice, things are different, and that is something else we'll look at in Chapter Two.

But, for now, just let's say that I certainly expected help from the Fourth Official if something difficult happened in my matches. I didn't always get that help, but there you go. Anyway, if I had been confronted by a 'goal' like Hurst's, I would walk very, very slowly towards the assistant referee and say, 'Did anyone else get a view?' With that cue, I would expect the Fourth Official urgently to seek a video replay. Then he would say, 'You can't tell Pollie.' Or, more likely, he would say, 'It's on the line Pollie. No goal.' That might not be legal, but it would ensure natural justice was served. Sorry, Sir Geoff. Sorry, England.

That is what a referee who took charge of World Cup matches in 2006 would have done in 1966, but Gottfried Dienst was the best referee of his day, because he was given the World Cup Final. And he did what all referees of that era would have done. So I am not criticizing him at all. I am not in a position to, am I?

As for our mate Bakhramov, well, the Germans have two versions of events. In one, they say that he claimed he thought Hurst's shot had hit the roof of the net (rather than the bar) before bouncing down. If that is true, then his eyesight was rubbish but there is no evidence that he said that and I don't think it is plausible that he did. It is much more likely that in the split second he had, and from the angle he had, he thought the ball had bounced down *over* the line. I am sure there must have been doubts in his mind. So he should not have said, 'Ye-es'. He should have said 'No-o'.

The second German legend is that, when Bakhramov was on his deathbed (he died in 1993) he was asked how he was sure the ball had crossed the line and is said to have replied, 'Stalingrad' (a reference to a bloody conflict in the Second World War – in which Germany laid siege to a city in the Soviet Union and there were tens of thousands of civilian casualties). The mere word 'Stalingrad' had a deep resonance for anyone from the old Soviet Bloc. The allegation is that Bakhramov was gaining revenge for his people. Again, there's no evidence that Bakhramov said that and I refuse to believe it.

As someone who was often enraged by unfair allegations about my refereeing, my instinct is to find Bakhramov innocent of German accusations of incompetence or deliberate unfairness.

What I do concede is that there is often a subconscious, subliminal tendency to favour the home team. Deep inside your brain, there is a little half-thought that giving a big decision against a noisy home crowd is difficult. Sometimes in those circumstances you hesitate, just momentarily. And once you have hesitated, you have effectively decided not to give the decision. Referees don't admit to the general public that this happens but it is only human nature. Good referees acknowledge this subliminal process and guard against it. Was Bakhramov proficient enough to ignore the pressure of the circumstances? Almost certainly not. With England playing at Wembley in the World Cup Final it would have been extremely difficult to give a goal *against* them if the ball bounced down from the crossbar. But it was relatively easy for Bakhramov to give the goal *for* England. I don't think he was deliberately biased. But it is possible he might have suffered from an unintentional, subconscious bias.

THE REF'S DECISION

One conclusion about 1966 springs from the lack of dissent shown after Bakhramov's momentous decision. He said it was a goal and, because there were no slo-mo replays, nobody knew any different. It was assumed that the linesman (and the referee) were right. Their decisions were final and were respected. Now, all close calls are disputed and the assumption is that the officials are wrong.

It would be a good thing if more people could remember that, down on the pitch, when nobody knows for certain what happened, everyone has to rely on a neutral arbiter: the ref or his assistant.

Another conclusion to be drawn from the 1966 goal is that some things have improved. As we have seen, language difficulties have been eradicated, specialist assistant refs are used, teams of officials come from the same country and are familiar with working with each other, they are 'wired for sound' and instructions to assistants have improved.

But the most worrying conclusion is that it could happen again. A World Cup Final could be decided by a 'goal' that is not a goal.

I'd like to think that I, or any modern, experienced, competent referee, would have helped to prevent the assistant from making such an obvious mistake. But you cannot rule out a similar, less blatant error without technology that accurately determines whether the ball has crossed the goal-line. Without technology, it will always be guesswork and there will always be wrong guesses. So, without question or quibble, football should develop and embrace goal-line technology.

As a referee or assistant, you make hundreds of judgements during a game and many of them are only opinions. Did that player handle the ball deliberately? Was that tackle reckless? All you can do is make an honest assessment and give your opinion. If, after the game, you find that some people – perhaps even most people – disagree with your opinion, that's up to them. You can still travel home content in the knowledge that all you did was give the best opinion you could in the circumstances.

But you also have to make judgements on matters of fact. Was that foul inside the penalty area? Did that shot cross the line? You can be proved right or wrong by television cameras – and if you get a big call wrong, you drive home cursing yourself. Football is about goals, so the biggest call you can make is whether a goal has been scored legitimately. If you get one of those calls wrong, it can eat away at your mind as you drive home.

The two rugby codes, Union and League, use video replays to decide whether tries have been scored legally. Cricket uses video replays for run-outs and has started using the Hawk-Eye computer system when there is an argument about whether the batsman was 'leg before' and when a 'caught behind' is disputed. Tennis adopted the Cyclops system of judging line calls, and then moved on to use of Hawk-Eye. I did some research on the tennis system for the BBC and found it fascinating that the players accepted Hawk-Eye was not always right. They accepted a certain degree of error from a machine.

Meanwhile, of all the major sports, only football refuses to use technology to solve disputes. We've done everything else that is possible, but not the one thing which would prevent mistakes. Nearly every referee I know would welcome accurate, efficient goal-line equipment – a 'beep' that announces, yes, the ball crossed the line. Only then could we be sure that a mistake as important as the one that allowed Hurst's goal to stand would not be repeated.

Without video technology, it is always possible a mistake will be made, and if an assistant referee says he is 100 per cent convinced that the ball has crossed the line, you have to take him at his word and award the goal. A referee has to rely on his assistants and, as old Bakhramov demonstrated all those years ago, sometimes assistants do funny things. As further proof of that, I'd like you to think about a highly contentious incident in the 2008/09 English season. Actually, no, it was not contentious because everyone knows what happened. Inexplicable is a better word. Inexcusable is another one.

On 20 September 2008, a very young referee, Stuart Attwell, awarded a goal to Reading at Watford in the Football League's top division. His assistant, Nigel Bannister, signalled the goal but should have flagged for a corner.

In the Laws of Football, which are set by FIFA, the game's world governing body, number ten deals with 'The Method of Scoring'. It states, 'A goal is scored when the whole of the ball passes over the goal line, between the goalposts and under the crossbar ...' So the incident had ticked some of the boxes – but not the important bit about between the goalposts! Bannister had been instructed to signal only for things about which he was absolutely certain. He had been told not to 'see' things that hadn't happened. Yet Bannister was convinced that he'd seen a goal scored. For whatever reason, he just had an aberration. When Attwell went over to talk to him, there was confusion between them about the specific moment to which

Bannister was referring, but he was a very experienced assistant and he was adamant that a goal had been scored, so the inexperienced Attwell was persuaded by the older man's certainty.

It was an extreme example – so extreme that, if repeated in a World Cup Final, I bet FIFA would go against their own rules and get a message to the ref to stop the goal being awarded. However, the clear lesson from Reading's 'phantom goal' is that errors do happen and, without video technology, they always will. In a less extreme case – for instance, when a ball bounces almost completely over the goal-line in the goal – it is very, very possible for the assistant and the ref to award a goal wrongly, even in a World Cup Final.

Of course, there would be one big difference if something similar to 1966 happened now – the poor referee will not be like Gottfried Dienst, who was allowed to continue the match without a word of protest and left the stadium unperturbed to get on with his life. Now, as soon as the incident happened, instant replays would be shown in the media areas of the stadium and all around the world. As two great mates of mine, top referees Urs Meier and Anders Frisk, learned to their cost, the reaction to controversial incidents is now extreme. I shall return to them later in this book, because they were very badly treated by 'fans' from England.

For now, though, I want to underline this conclusion from our consideration of the 1966 goal: something very similar could happen again. All these years have passed, so much has been improved, yet it could happen again. It could happen in 2010. I find that frightening. And next time, it could be England on the wrong end of a wrong decision.

WORLD CUP STATS: 1966

QUALIFICATION TOURNAMENT: African nations boycotted the tournament because FIFA had stipulated that the continent's top team should play off against the winners from Asia or Oceana for a place in the finals. The 70 teams that did contest the qualifying tournament were a record. England were given a place in the finals as hosts. None of the other home nations qualified. Germany had been divided into two separate countries after the Second World War. West Germany were among ten European teams in the finals.

FINALS: 11–30 July. The sixteen teams were divided into four groups of four. The top two from each team progressed to the quarter-finals.

HOSTS: England

MASCOT: World Cup Willie (the first World Cup mascot: a lion on his hind legs, wearing a union flag shirt)

FINAL: England 4, West Germany 2 (after extra-time)

MATCHES PLAYED: 32

GOALS SCORED: 89

ATTENDANCE: 1,635,000

TOP SCORER: Eusebio (Portugal, 9 goals)

HOME NATIONS: England played all their matches at Wembley, which gave them a huge advantage. They started slowly, with a goalless game against Uruguay, and only scored four goals in their group matches. Significantly, they did not concede a goal until the semi-final, in which they beat Portugal. The story of the Final is told in this chapter.

MOURINHO'S GHOST

Down the years since 1966 there have been many, many other controversies about whether the ball entered the goal. One of the most contentious was when Luis Garcia scored for Liverpool against Chelsea in the European Champions League semi-final on 3 May 2005. Did his shot cross the line before Chelsea's William Gallas hooked it away? The match officials said 'Yes'. José Mourinho, who was Chelsea's manager, remains adamant to this day that it was 'a ghost goal, a goal from the moon'.

I've got some history with Senhor Mourinho, but I'll try to be impartial – as I can assure you and him I always was when I refereed teams he managed. The ref that night at Anfield was Lubos Michel from Slovakia, whom I know well. We were at two World Cups together. He was one of the top men in refereeing and by 2005 he had already been on the international list for a dozen years – and he had refereed a big match involving Mourinho two years earlier. That was the UEFA Cup Final between Mourinho's Porto and Celtic on 21 May 2003. Martin O'Neill, the Celtic manager at the time, criticized Michel for sending off one of his players and allowing Porto to get away with some time-wasting. Funnily enough, Mourinho had no complaints.

Funnily enough as well, in 2005 he did not comment on what happened immediately before the 'ghost goal'. Liverpool's Milan Baros clipped the ball up over the advancing goalkeeper, Petr Cech, but was flattened by him. Garcia nipped in and knocked the ball goalwards. The assistant referee, Michel's compatriot Roman Slysko, was well positioned and instantly signalled a goal. Bearing in mind what I've told you about referees' instructions to assistants, we can be sure that Slysko was certain the ball had crossed the line.

But Michel still had to make the decision. I've asked him about it. He told me, 'Either it was a goal – and my assistant was sure it was – or I had to give a penalty against Petr Cech and send him off for denying a clear goal-scoring opportunity. I believe Chelsea would have preferred the goal to count rather than face a penalty and have ten men for the rest of the game.'

So, yes, I'd say justice was done. UEFA, the game's governing body in Europe, obviously had no problem with either Michel or Slysko. They were appointed together for the 2008 Champions League Final in Moscow. Mourinho had been sacked by then but Chelsea lost that one as well.

You remember that it was William Gallas who hooked away Garcia's shot. Well, Gallas was the beneficiary of a goal-line decision on 3 November 2007 when he was playing for Arsenal against

Manchester United at the Emirates. United were leading 2–1 but, in added time, Gallas shot and United goalkeeper Edwin van der Sar pawed the ball away. Assistant referee Darren Cann was perfectly placed to make a decision and brave enough to do so. He signalled that the ball had crossed the line. He was correct.

It takes courage to make a big decision at a crucial moment, and a very skilled person to get a difficult decision right in those circumstances. I'd cite Cann's call as the best of the 2007/08 season. To me, that is a perfect illustration of how hard the job of an assistant is.

But, no, they don't always get it right. And that brings us to the incident involving Pedro Mendes of Spurs and Roy Carroll of Manchester United at Old Trafford on 4 January 2005. Mendes definitely scored a goal for Spurs. But he shot from way out and assistant referee Rob Lewis was 20 yards or so upfield. He could not see when the ball entered the goal. Nor could referee Mark Clattenburg. So, when Carroll clawed the ball away from more than a yard behind the line, everyone played on. Spurs reckon the officials' mistake cost the London club a place in the Champions League because it robbed them of a win and two points. That is how many they finished behind fourth-placed Arsenal in the table. Mind you, they did drop 51 points in other matches!

Similarly, can Bolton really claim to have been relegated in the 1997/98 Premiership season because of one goal-line decision? Of course not. They only collected 40 points all season. Yet you can understand why they were aggrieved when Everton survived on goal-difference, because earlier in the season, at the Reebok stadium, Gerry Taggart had thought he'd scored for Bolton to beat Everton but referee Stephen Lodge could not see whether the ball had crossed the line and so did not award a goal. That match was on 1 September 1997.

A little under five months earlier, an event occurred which the people of Chesterfield believe was the biggest miscarriage of justice in FA Cup history. On 13 April 1997, Chesterfield, from the third tier of English football, were 2–1 up in the semi-final against Middlesbrough, from the top division. Chesterfield's Jonathan Howard crashed a shot against the bar and believed that it bounced down over the line. The assistant, Alan Sheffield, thought so as well and signalled a goal. I have explained that referees do not want assistants to 'see' things that have not happened, but in this example, the assistant was correct. TV replays showed that the ball was, indeed, over the line. The assistant had the courage of his convictions, signalled and ran back towards the halfway line. Yet referee David Elleray did not award the goal. Middlesbrough fans claimed that Elleray had already blown for a foul against a Middlesbrough player. Elleray denied that. He said he was merely unsighted and so could not award the goal. Sheffield was an international assistant, but Elleray did not take his word for what had happened. The other assistant was Phil Sharp. I asked both him and Sheffield about the incident but they told me they had been instructed by Elleray not to discuss it.

The match ended 3–3. Middlesbrough won the replay. Chesterfield's chance of an historic Final appearance had gone. So don't try telling anyone in Derbyshire that justice was served.

OUR FINEST REF ... AND ME

England's George Courtney went to the World Cup in 1986 and 1990. He was one of the finest referees this country has ever produced, and a hero to me. But his preparation for those World Cups shows why the system of sending specialist assistant referees to major competitions is an improvement on what used to happen.

Only referees were sent to the World Cups of 1986 and 1990, so George had to take his turns as a linesman. He was a truly great referee, but hadn't operated regularly as a linesman for years. In the build-up to both of his World Cups, he was given a handful of domestic games as a linesman, to try to re-familiarize himself with the job. But that merely underlines that the authorities accepted that he was out of practice.

George, a lovely man, was the referee in 1991 when I made my first ever international trip. We travelled to Rotterdam, for a Euro 92 qualifier between Holland and Portugal. I was one of George's assistants and delighted to be chosen, but I was a Football League referee by then and decidedly rusty at running the line.

WHEN LINESMEN CAME ... AND WENT

THE role of linesman is as old as football, but when the game was first played, the linesmen were not neutrals; they were spare players or other people associated with the two teams. That is still the case in much parks football and other 'grass roots' matches.

Originally, if a 'lino' saw any offence, he stuck up his flag and play had to stop. But the 1891 Laws of Football changed all that and made it clear that linesmen were only there to assist the referee, and that it was the ref who decided when to stop play. The 1891 Laws gave linesmen very limited powers and duties. Four years later, by which time some linesmen were neutral, a new edition of the Laws gave them more responsibility, but again made it clear that they were referees' helpers.

The title 'linesman' was changed to 'assistant referee' for the start of the 1996/97 season, partly because there were many more lines*women* by then and partly because the authorities wanted recognition for the fact that linesmen and women were expected to do more to help the ref than just wave their flags from time to time.

FLAGGING, NOT WAVING

YOU will hear commentators say that an assistant has flagged for offside when it turns out to be for a foul, and vice versa. That's because they don't know the different signals.

For a foul, the assistant stands with the flag pointing along the touchline in the direction the free-kick will be taken.

For offside, he (or she) stands with the flag pointing towards the pitch – high in the air if the offside player was on the other side of the pitch, parallel with the ground if the offence was halfway across the pitch, and at an angle with the ground if the offence was on the assistant's side of the field.

There are other, less conspicuous signals as well, especially at games below the level where there is radio communication. For instance, if an assistant is not sure which way to give a throw-in, he or she will wait until the referee has pointed with a finger or hand – subtly, almost imperceptibly. Then the assistant will not fall into the trap of signalling one direction and being overruled.

If it appears that there is disagreement between the referee and an assistant, there is far more likely to be dissent from players and abuse from spectators, so it is important for officials to avoid appearing to disagree. It is also important to remember that the ref is the one who makes the decisions. So, sometimes, assistants don't signal for offences. Spectators and commentators will say, 'The linesman must have seen that.' But if the assistant knows that the ref has got a good view of an incident, it is not the assistant's job to signal. It is good practice to leave it to the referee, because he might want to play an 'advantage'.

YELLOW CARD FOR FIFA

THE fact that Tofik Bakhramov was the top man in Azerbaijan did not guarantee he was especially proficient as a referee, let alone as a linesman. FIFA feel obliged to appoint officials from all over the globe for World Cups, to encourage referees in every country. That means you don't get the best officials.

If there were no considerations other than assembling the 20 finest refs, you would get eight or ten from Europe and six or seven from South America. Other than a few occasional, outstanding exceptions, the best referees come from countries with top-standard leagues and demanding matches. Yet at World Cups, there are always referees and assistants from smaller footballing nations with limited experience of really big games.

RED CARD FOR PLATINI

THERE have been very successful experiments on football goal-line technology by Hawk-Eye, the company which makes equipment which is accepted in tennis and is used in television coverage of cricket. The experiments, conducted at Fulham and Reading, were proposed by the Premier League and sanctioned by FIFA. Yet, in March 2008, the International Football Association Board (FIFA's Laws committee) decreed that the experiments must end. They were persuaded by a 'strongly-worded intervention' from the president of UEFA, Michel Platini. He believes that, once you introduce any technology at all, you open Pandora's box.

Platini was a wonderful player for France and Juventus and his election as president of UEFA in January 2007 made him the top administrator in Europe. His election was hailed by football folk because, at last, a former player was to be one of the game's leaders. But, the next time your team is denied a good goal because the assistant referee did not see that the ball crossed the line, don't blame the assistant and don't blame the ref. The person you should blame is Michel Platini.

NO MORE YES MEN

FROM the year 2000, to reduce 'Ye-es' moments, FIFA imposed some additional, standardized instructions for assistant referees.

If the ref signals for a foul near the penalty area and the assistant is sure it was *outside* the box, the assistant should take an exaggerated step towards the halfway line. If the assistant is certain the foul was *inside* the area, he should run towards the corner flag.

FIFA do not want referees going over to talk to assistants, because that would look as if the ref is unsure about the decision and the players would surround the officials to have their say.

In my autobiography, *Seeing Red*, I recount an incident just like that in Euro 2000. I took charge of a match between the Czech Republic and France on 16 June in Bruges. Despite those careful, homogenized instructions on what to do about penalty decisions, I still went over to my assistant, Eddie Foley from Cork, to find out what had happened. We gave a penalty instead of a free-kick outside the area. We got the decision wrong. And UEFA were not happy that I had ignored the directive.

LANGUAGE PROBLEM

Dave Bryan was one of the best assistant referees I worked with, but he had his own '66 moment on 3 January 2004, when he signalled for a goal by Watford's Heidar Helguson against Chelsea. The ball hit the bar and bounced down on – or, according to Dave, over – the line.

He had his language difficulties when he was on foreign trips. On one occasion, at a match in Macedonia, the assessor was German and the officials were English. They included Dave, plus Mike Dean and Steve Dunn, who are big mates of mine. One of them asked the assessor his profession. He said, 'I am ein doctair. I work with children. I am a paedi ... paedi ...'

As he struggled for the English word paediatrician, Dave tried to help out. 'Paedophile?' he offered, unthinkingly. Steve and Mike fell off their chairs laughing.

YELLOW CARD FOR ROB

THE Mendes–Carroll goal (at Old Trafford on 4 January 2005) was such a blatantly wrong decision that referee Mark Clattenburg and assistant Rob Lewis beat themselves up about it. I spoke to Mark very soon afterwards and told him it wasn't his fault and that nobody blamed him, but he was very upset because it was so clearly a goal.

Interestingly, though, at the time, Sky television's commentators were not sure until they'd seen a replay. That is what often happens. Once we've all seen a dozen replays of an incident, we convince ourselves that what happened was obvious. Mark and Rob didn't have any replays and had to go on what they'd seen at the time. The problem was that Rob didn't give himself a chance of seeing anything much. He went into sprint mode, belting along the line to try to get back closer to the goal, and his head went down as he ran. It is easy to be critical with hindsight, but instead of racing back quite so frantically, Rob should have concentrated on the flight of the ball. So I think there is a good learning point from the Mendes–Carroll goal. It is that there are times when, as a referee or assistant, you have to accept that you must sacrifice proximity for viewing angle.

You have to keep an awareness of what is going on and what might be about to happen, and so you will notice good referees sometimes stop running forwards and take a step to one side to get a better angle. Similarly, an assistant should cover the ground as quickly as possible but while maintaining a good view. The assistant's two main functions are to watch for offsides and to indicate when the ball goes out of play. As soon as Mendes hit his shot, there was no possibility of an offside and so Rob could and should have concentrated on 'ball out of play'. With hindsight he knows he should have focused on the ball and the possibility that it would go into the goal.

RED CARD FOR POLL

I HAVE my own reason for remembering the name of the 'Russian' linesman, Tofik Bakhramov. As I have explained, he was really from Azerbaijan. The top stadium in that country is named after him. I refereed my first full international match there on 2 April 1997 (not, as some of you might imagine, the day before). I remember clearly that there was a sign showing a picture of a Kalashnikov with a cross through it, instructing everyone to leave rifles outside the stadium. You don't see that in this country. Not since Millwall moved from the old Den.

I remember clearly that my match in the Tofik Bakhramov Stadium was a World Cup qualifier between Azerbaijan and Finland, and that the home side lost 2–1. What I don't remember with any clarity is the hospitality afterwards, because instead of the few beers we were hoping for, the officials were given double shots of vodka.

Our hosts kept toasting us. Me and Steve Dunn (who was my Fourth Official again) kept replying to the toasts. Every time we did so, our glasses were refilled. After about 15 double vodkas, we realized that they wouldn't stop toasting us until we stopped toasting them. By then we could barely walk.

Finland had won the match. If Azerbaijan had won, the toasting would never have stopped. We'd still be there knocking back the doubles. But then all Englishmen should be happy to raise a glass to Bakhramov, the man whose decision won us the World Cup.

FACT! THE THIRD MAN

THE 'Russian' linesman and referee Gottfried Dienst are well remembered, but who was the other linesman? He was Karol Galba, from what was then known as Czecho-slovakia. He had refereed one match at the 1962 World Cup and went on to be the first president of the UEFA referees' committee. In 2006, when the new Wembley stadium was being built, a ceremony was held on the pitch to mark the fortieth anniversary of the 1966 Final. Galba, the only surviving match official, attended, along with players from both sides.

2

ZIDANE HEADS FOR THE DRESSING ROOM

THE MATCH

Was video evidence used to 'convict' the world's greatest player in the world's biggest fixture? That is the question I find myself asking the more I think about the 2006 World Cup Final.

The best player in the world? That was Zinedine Zidane. He'd won that title three times. He also won the World Cup with France, in Paris in 1998, and the European Championship two years later. He helped Juventus to two successive European Champions League finals and became the world's most expensive player when he joined Real Madrid for 76 million euros. He scored the winning goal when the Spanish club won the Champions League. It was a remarkable career and it was to have an extraordinary conclusion.

In May 2006 he announced that he would retire after that year's World Cup. So, when his beloved France reached the Final, it meant that the finest footballer on the planet was going to play his last competitive match in the globe's biggest game. Nobody of his stature had ever chosen such a prestigious stage for his last bow. But, on the day, he made his exit as the villain, sent off for violent conduct. What an incredible story.

Yet is the full story even more intriguing? Like many others in refereeing circles, I cannot help wondering whether the officials used video technology against Zidane in Berlin's Olympiastadion on 9 July 2006. If I had been the referee or the Fourth Official in those precise circumstances, then I would have wanted to get it right. And if that meant using a TV replay to check what had happened, so be it. Did the men in charge of the match do that? Has technology already been used in the world's most important fixture?

What we can say for certain is that if 'Zizou' had been able to control his temper as well as he could control a football then none of this would be an issue. If he had been able to keep his head, instead of using it as a weapon, he might well have provided a much more fitting finish to his peerless career. He was the captain of France and there is a real possibility that he could have completed his playing days by lifting the World Cup. Instead, the last sight of him as a professional footballer was as he walked past the trophy on his way back to the dressing room after being sent off.

The 2006 World Cup Final pitched France against Italy and the two players who were to feature later in the most controversial confrontation each scored in the first 20 minutes. In fact, those two men, Zidane and Marco Materazzi, were both involved in the first goal, after seven minutes. It was Materazzi who fouled France's Florent Malouda (although there was only the most minimal contact) and it was Zidane who converted the penalty to put France ahead.

Zidane being Zidane, the penalty was a bit special. As goalkeeper Gianluigi Buffon sprawled to his right, expecting a normal, hard shot, Zidane chipped the ball and sent it forwards and upwards in a slow parabola. Buffon was already on the floor long before the ball lazily clipped the underside of the bar and bounced down. He clambered up, turned around, and grabbed the ball but there was no need for an Azerbaijani assistant referee to decide that it had clearly crossed the line.

Thirteen minutes later, Materazzi equalized, leaping two feet higher than his marker to head home an Andrea Pirlo corner, and it was still 1–1 after 90 minutes.

Fourteen minutes into extra-time, goalkeeper Buffon tipped a Zidane header over the bar, but the French captain's next, and last, contribution to the beautiful game was a moment of ugly bad temper. Angered by something Materazzi said to him, Zidane head-butted the Italian defender in the chest. It was a belting butt. Materazzi went down like a felled tree. He was hurt, no doubt, but probably also stunned – and so was the watching world when TV showed the astonishing incident. But that didn't happen straightaway. It was an off-the-ball clash and TV coverage was following the ball. So there was quite a lot of confusion until a replay of the incident made it apparent that Zidane deserved to be sent off.

There was confusion as well for the referee, Horacio Elizondo from Argentina. He had also been concentrating on the ball and hadn't seen the head-butt. It is how he learned that Zidane deserved to be sent off that fascinates me. That is what is still discussed and debated in refereeing circles. But, for now, let's just say that Elizondo did get the message and did show Zidane the red card. For me, watching at home, the sight of the best player I ever refereed walking back to the dressing room and passing the World Cup, where it stood on a plinth waiting for the presentation ceremony, was one of the saddest moments I can remember; sad for a player I admired so much and sad for football.

There were no more goals. So, for only the second time, the World Cup Final was decided by penalties. Materazzi took Italy's second spot-kick, and scored. David Trezeguet, the man whose goal gave France victory over Italy in the Final of Euro 2000, was the only player not to score his penalty. His kick hit the crossbar, landed on the goal-line and bounced out. Again, no Azerbaijani assistant was needed. It was not a goal. Italy won the penalty contest 5–3, and with it their fourth World Cup.

THE ISSUES

I am intrigued by what happened after the clash between Zidane and Materazzi. But what happened immediately before it, and provoked it, has also been the subject of controversy ever since.

France were attacking. Both men were standing in the Italian penalty area with their backs to the goal. The Italian was immediately behind the Frenchman and, as happens more often than not in modern football, grabbed hold of him. He stretched his right arm around in front of Zidane and grabbed a handful of shirt at about – if you'll pardon the expression – nipple height.

The attack broke down, the ball sailed forward over their heads, Materazzi let go of Zidane and both men strolled forward towards the halfway line. Words were exchanged. Both men agree about the beginning of the exchange. They concur that, when Materazzi had hold of Zidane, the Frenchman said, 'If you want my shirt that badly, I shall give it to you after the match.' What was said next has been disputed, and Materazzi won damages from a British newspaper which alleged, falsely, that he used a racist expression. So let's accept Materazzi's version, which appeared in his autobiography.

Materazzi wrote that he was upset by Zidane's tone, which the Italian felt implied he was not worthy of receiving such an important shirt. 'Because I was annoyed by his arrogance, I replied, "*Preferisco la puttana di tua sorella*" (I would rather have your whore of a sister).'

Nice. So Zidane turned, put his head down like a bull about to charge, and rammed Materazzi with it.

After the match, whenever the sending off was shown on television, you saw Zidane head-butt Materazzi and then referee Elizondo sprinting over and brandishing his red card. But that was an edited clip and not how it happened. One minute and thirty seconds passed between the violent conduct and the red card, and it is what happened during that minute and a half that intrigues me.

The referee did not see the incident. Neither did either of the assistants. That much was agreed afterwards and, anyway, if the ref had seen the head-butt, he would have stopped play at once and sent off Zidane much sooner. Similarly, if an assistant had seen it, he would have flagged straightaway, pressed the buzzer on his flag to alert the ref and have spoken into his lip microphone, saying something like, 'Stop play! There's been a head-butt.' We know that didn't happen.

Play went on briefly and only stopped when referee Elizondo awarded a free-kick to France near the halfway line for an entirely different, minor incident more than 30 metres away from the head-butt. At that point, Elizondo became aware of Materazzi flat out on the grass and ran over to him. The ref did not talk to Zidane at all, but called on the trainer to deal with the injury. Players milled around. Buffon, the Italian goalkeeper, came out of his area to join in and made a gesture to the nearest assistant referee, pointing at his own eye as if to say, 'You must have seen that.' Eventually Elizondo jogged over to that assistant and had a very, very brief conversation. Neither man said more than four or five words. After that, Elizondo sprinted back to Zidane and sent him off.

The next day FIFA released a statement. The crucial part said, 'The incident was directly observed [i.e., without the use of a monitor] by Fourth Official Luis Medina Cantalejo from his position at the pitchside, who informed the referee and his assistants through the communications system.'

That authorized version of events was important to FIFA because they were, and are, stubbornly opposed to the use of video replays or similar technological help for referees. FIFA's position is that it is a Pandora's box which must never be opened. Their belief is that if you allow the use of technology to help decide whether the ball has crossed the goal-line for a goal, for instance, then the pressure would increase to use slow-motion replays to review penalty decisions, sendings off, offsides ... and almost everything.

I have asked myself what I would have done. That is what referees usually think when something controversial happens in a football match. It's part of the learning process, part of the self-appraisal that goes on all the time. Sometimes, as well, you have a special reason for putting yourself in the shoes of the ref. For instance, when I was sent home early from Euro 2000, I could not help calculating that, if I'd stayed and things had gone well, my last match would probably have been the semi-final between France and Portugal. So I watched with special interest when that match ended in incredible drama. There was a handball on the line in extra-time. It led to a sending off and a penalty – and the spot-kick won the match for France because the 'golden goal' rule applied at the time (the first goal scored in extra-time won the match). I sat and watched that all unfold and kept thinking, 'Blimey! I might have had to give those critical decisions.'

And again on 9 July 2006, as I watched the World Cup Final on TV at my home in Tring, Hertfordshire, I had an additional reason for putting myself in the place of the ref – because, if I had not made my three yellow cards mistake, it might have been me refereeing the Final. So, yes, I thought what I would have done – what I should have done – if I had been the ref. And if I had been the referee, I hope I would have prevented the confrontation between Zidane and Materazzi.

As you run back following play, you are sometimes aware of men having a go at each other. You get a feel, a sense, of things like that from the body language, from the circumstances and from experience. Then, you ask yourself whether you can trust them not to let their squabble get out of hand. If the answer is, 'No', then you stop play, go over and say, 'Lads, have you got a problem?' You manage them and the situation, and it all blows over.

Referee Elizondo didn't do any of that, so perhaps he saw nothing untoward as he ran away from the Italian area. So what about the assistant? Again, sitting at home, I put myself in his position. As the assistant, I would be very grateful to the referee. It was the ref who was selected for the World Cup, so I would know I owed my role on the big day to him and would be in his debt for the rest of my life. I would certainly want to repay him by assisting him to the very best of my ability and by trying to ensure that the match passed without any mistakes. So I would have been very disappointed with myself if I'd missed the head-butt.

The assistant's job, as the ball was cleared, was to consider whether there was likely to be an offside if the ball was pumped back into the box. He needed to be in line with the second last defender (the last defender was the goalkeeper, don't forget). And the assistant should have been looking along the line of players. Like the referee, he too should have had a sense, a feeling, when something was about to kick off. Yet, according to FIFA's statement, it was only the Fourth Official who saw the head-butt.

So I put myself in the shoes – boots rather – of the Fourth Official, Luis Medina Cantalejo, with whom I'd spent some time during my period at that World Cup, and who I liked very much. We went on a couple of bike rides together, to break the monotony of life in 'camp' and to help maintain our fitness. He was a good thinker and an interesting talker. He was an upright, very correct man and very experienced. I would have been absolutely delighted if he had been my Fourth Official for any match, including the World Cup Final.

The Fourth Official does not have much to do. One of his duties is to tell the ref if the same player has been cautioned twice but not sent off (as if!). He might also notify the referee if there is a minor altercation between a couple of players. In those circumstances, he would not intervene immediately, but when there is a stoppage he'd say to the ref, 'You might like to have a word with Zidane and Materazzi. They were at it a minute ago.' That is good, supportive work from the Fourth Official, quietly helping the referee. But Zidane's head-butt was much more serious than that and demanded a more vigorous response.

One of the three games my friend Luis had refereed in the 2006 World Cup was the match on 26 June between Italy and Australia – in which he sent off Materazzi. In the Final, if he had seen that same man floored by the world's greatest player, do you suppose he would have sat around twiddling his thumbs? If it had been me, I would have been straight on my lip mike and said, 'I say Horacio, there's been violent conduct out of your view' – or words to that effect. Yet one minute and thirty seconds elapsed after the head-butt while the players were milling around the stricken Italian and Zidane. And, sitting at home in Tring, I thought, 'Nobody saw it! Nobody can have seen it!'

Perhaps Luis had been doing some paperwork, or talking to the FIFA delegate – as you do – when the head-butt happened. Perhaps he saw something in his peripheral vision, looked up and saw Materazzi on the floor. In those circumstances, I would have expected my experience to have told me from Zidane's posture that he was the culprit. I would have said to the assistant referee, 'Did he just hit him?' And I would have looked at the TV monitor near me for a replay, urgently.

I believe that if I had been the Fourth Official it would have been right to turn to look at the TV, in terms of natural justice and the spirit of football. Zidane and I had a good relationship and I loved refereeing matches in which he played. But he deserved to be sent off against Italy in the World Cup Final. If he had escaped punishment, the World Cup would have ended in farce, because everyone would have known that there had been a major injustice. And think of the implications if, after getting away with his crime, Zidane had scored the winning goal. Certainly, at the time, implications like that would have been going through the minds of every FIFA man and woman at the Final.

At home in Tring, I put myself in all the refereeing roles. I played out all the scenarios in my mind. In my versions, they all ended with the Fourth Official using the TV replay.

THE REF'S DECISION

What I conclude from the 2006 Final is that, despite FIFA's protestations about not allowing video replays, technology or anything to intrude on the sanctity of the referee's decision-making on the pitch, there are times when a more pragmatic approach is called for.

The alternative view is that it would be OK to allow a serious error to be made in a World Cup Final – a mistake which would be known by anyone and everyone watching a television, but not by the referee out there in the middle of the pitch.

Think about the two most flagrant examples of mistakes about goals of recent years, both considered in the previous chapter. They were Reading's 'phantom goal' at Watford on 20 September 2008 (when the ball went wide of the posts yet a goal was awarded) and the incident involving Pedro Mendes of Spurs at Old Trafford on 4 January 2005 (when his shot clearly entered the goal but no goal was given). If something like either of those were to happen in a World Cup Final, surely FIFA should ensure that the Fourth Official was aware of it and that he alerted the referee straightaway, even if that meant not sticking rigidly and pedantically to their rules about using TV replays.

My contention is that FIFA would be sensible and put the credibility of their competition ahead of a narrow-minded adherence to rules. Violent conduct that the referee misses should not be allowed to go unpunished, just as Zidane did not get away with it in 2006. I also believe, 100 per cent, that FIFA should prevent a reoccurrence of what happened to me in 2006 – and I suspect that they will never let it happen again.

I accept total responsibility for showing my yellow card three times to Croatia defender Josip Simunic, instead of sending him off after two. But if it happens again to some other poor sap, and if, as in my case, neither of the referee's assistants nor the Fourth Official realizes, then someone with access to the television coverage will respond. A message will be sent to the Fourth Official, and, through him, to the ref. I am convinced about that, because my mistake caused FIFA such embarrassment.

I have another conclusion from the Zidane scenario and it is this. If we can envisage situations when FIFA would be forced to consult TV replays (even if they look at them surreptitiously) then why pretend otherwise? Why do they say, not only 'No technology' but also 'No experiments on technology'? Why do nothing, when they could really do something open and helpful? It is madness.

WORLD CUP STATS: 2006

QUALIFICATION TOURNAMENT: This was the first World Cup in which the holders were not given automatic qualification to the finals. Germany were guaranteed a place as hosts but 198 teams contested the remaining 31 places.

FINALS: 9 June to 9 July. The thirty-two teams were divided into eight groups of four. The eight group winners and the eight group runners-up qualified for three rounds of knock-out matches which produced two finalists.

HOSTS: Germany

MASCOTS: Goleo (A lion wearing a Germany shirt with the number 06) and Pille (a talking football)

FINAL: Italy 1, France 1 (after extra-time), Italy won 5–3 on penalties

MATCHES PLAYED: 64

GOALS SCORED: 147

ATTENDANCE: 23,353,655

TOP SCORER: Mirolsav Klose (Germany, 6 goals)

HOME NATIONS: England, the only home nation to reach the finals, did so as winners of their qualifying group. In Germany they were unconvincing in wins against Paraguay and Trinidad and Tobago (the smallest country ever to have reached the finals). A draw against Sweden was sufficient for England to top their group again, however, and they were 1–0 winners in the round of 16 match against Ecuador. In their quarter-final they were beaten on penalties by Portugal.

YELLOW CARD FOR THE LAW

WHAT do the Laws of the Game say about Fourth Officials? Nothing at all. They are not mentioned in the 17 actual Laws. But there is a page devoted to them in the additional information section in the booklet of the Laws of the Game. It says, the Fourth Official 'must indicate to the referee when the wrong player is cautioned because of mistaken identity or when a player is not sent off having been given a second caution, or when violent conduct occurs out of the view of the referee and assistant referees.'

Note that it does not say that the Fourth Official has to see the violent conduct with his own eyes. There is nothing in the letter of the Law which stipulates that the Fourth Official cannot consult a TV replay. In fact, there is nothing anywhere

in the Laws, or in any of the additional information, which mentions TV replays at all, let alone specifically precludes their use.

SLOW WAY TO SUCCEED

Zinedine Zidane's jibe about giving his shirt to Marco Materazzi started the verbal exchange which ended with the Italian flat on the floor, but the Frenchman gave me one of his shirts without a fight – although not without some shameless begging on my part. I tell the story in *Seeing Red*, so now let me just say that the shirt is on the wall of my study in my home, in Tring, in Hertfordshire (guarded by Toffee, our dog, in case you were wondering).

I am immensely proud to have that shirt because, regardless of how his career ended, 'Zizou' was a wonderful player. I am proud of the fact that I was considered good enough to referee several games in which he took part. I am very lucky that I was able to see his sublime skills at close hand.

It is said that great players have more time on the ball and in my experience that is certainly true. In Zidane's case, the extra time came from his anticipation, his speed of thought and his great technical ability. Before a pass reached him, he had already looked and thought ahead. He knew what he would do when the ball got to him. And when it did reach him, there was no fumbling or dithering. His first touch was sufficient to control the ball or to move it on in the direction he wanted it to go.

All of that meant that, although the modern game is played at a frenetic pace, Zidane had an unhurried tranquillity. When he wasn't nutting people, of course.

Good referees also try to give themselves time. They try to anticipate where and when incidents will happen, and try to think in advance about giving themselves a good view of those incidents. Then, when something happens, they try to give themselves a moment to think before reacting.

THE RELUCTANT VIEWER

The 2006 World Cup Final in Berlin was the one I might have refereed and then became the one I didn't want to watch.

I certainly didn't expect to referee it, or even allow myself to hope I would, but I now know that, if I had not made my infamous mistake with three yellow cards, there was a strong possibility that I might have been selected for the Final. Instead, I was sent home before the quarter-finals and was in such terrible, black despair that I did not think I would watch any of the remaining games. I didn't think I would be able to bear watching. But people – friends and family – said, 'You were there. You were part of that tournament. You've got no reason not to see how it finishes.'

And the day I got back from Germany to the safe harbour of my home in Tring, the very first telephone call I received was from David Beckham. The England captain was preparing for a World Cup quarter-final but took time to telephone me, empathizing with me in my desperate unhappiness and reaching out in friendship to me and my family. So I decided I definitely wanted to see Becks and the boys in action against Portugal.

Having been in Germany, where the people had been fantastic and the atmosphere fabulous, I was conscious of an overriding sense that the Germans were going to win. The World Cup was a statement of nationhood for the united Germany, and winning it seemed to be their destiny. I decided I definitely wanted to see their quarter-final against Argentina. Then I realized I wanted to watch Italy against Ukraine, because I've always loved Italian football. And of course I wanted to watch France against Brazil, because those countries have produced some of the best players to walk the earth.

So that was all the quarter-finals I had to watch, and by the time the Final came around, I was hooked on the beautiful game again and the great unscripted drama of the World Cup.

THE FIRST AND LAST REFEREE

The referee who sent off Zinedine Zidane in the 2006 World Cup Final, Horacio Elizondo from Argentina, was also in charge of the tournament's opening match, and that was remarkable.

The man who does the opening game (which is itself regarded as a great honour) has never before been given the Final as well. In fact, if you get the opening game, it is usually a clear indication that you are not going to get the Final.

When the referees all reported for duty in 2006, Mario van der Ende, one of the FIFA referees' committee guys from Holland, asked me what games I hoped to get. I said, 'The opening game would be nice.' His reply was, 'Why would you want that one? That would mean that you won't do the Final.'

Those in the European delegation were quite pleased when Elizondo from Argentina was appointed for the opening game. They believed that if a South American had been given that fixture, it was more likely that a European would get the Final. That was the logic. That was the politics.

Yet Elizondo did the first and last games in 2006. He did something else as well: he refereed England's quarter-final against Portugal and sent off Wayne Rooney. In all, he refereed five games. Again, that was unheard of before 2006.

I had not met Elizondo, I don't believe, before we met up during the tournament, and even then we didn't bump into each other very often. His English was very, very poor and he tended to stick with the guys who spoke Spanish. I do know that he was a PE teacher, was the same age as me and that he retired from refereeing soon after the World Cup Final.

That last fact interests me. Elizondo retired six years before he needed to because he had achieved all his goals. That makes me think that my dad was right when he said that what happened to me in Germany made no difference to my retirement. Whether I had messed up (as I did) or refereed the Final (as I might have done) I would have had the same feeling – that my race was run – and would have stopped refereeing at the same time.

RULES NOT FIT FOR PURPOSE

THE Fourth Official for the 2006 Final was, as I have said, Luis Medina Cantalejo. Liverpool supporters should know that name, because he was the man who gave their team a controversial penalty for a foul on Steven Gerrard in the last seconds of a Champions League match against Atletico Madrid in 2008.

He went to the 2006 World Cup because another Spaniard, Mejuto Gonzalez, was ruled out when one of the assistants in his team failed the fitness test. If FIFA had been selecting the top referees in the world, without worrying about giving every federation a share, then Luis would have been chosen in the first place. But imagine the disappointment for Gonzalez, after all the years of working and hoping, to be denied the chance to officiate in a World Cup because someone else was not fit.

YELLOW CARD FOR FOURTH OFFICIALS

AS mentioned previously, the role of the Fourth Official was only introduced in 1991. Before that time, there were reserve officials named for major matches but they played no part at all unless the referee or one of his linesmen (as they were then) suffered illness or injury.

A lot of people question the need for Fourth Officials, and to some extent I understand and share their doubts. Do we really need a guy to hold a board up to show the numbers of substitutes and how many minutes are being added on by the referee at the end of each half? Why can't that information be displayed on the big screens at most grounds?

Similarly, does the Fourth Official really have to keep jumping up to enforce the rules of the technical area – that there is only one person from each team standing in his area at any one time, and so on? All that policing the technical areas achieves is to aggravate the managers and fans and make the Fourth Official seem like a busybody. In theory, the Fourth Official is supposed to watch for and report any 'improper conduct' by managers and coaches, but so much of that goes on at every game that most is not reported.

I hated being the Fourth Official. You travel up to a hotel the night before the match, yet you know you are not one of the main officials. It's like being the substitute goalkeeper: you get all the kit on but then sit there knowing you don't have a proper part to play. It's very frustrating.

I don't think some other referees were too keen having me as their Fourth Official. It was all right if it was a really big game – say Arsenal against Manchester United – because then the referee concerned would be a top man and would not have a problem with me being there. He would know that I would sort out anything that really needed sorting in the technical area and let him get on with his job.

The problems arose sometimes when, in common with other senior match officials, I was appointed Fourth Official to mentor a young ref. Then the managers would sometimes talk to me instead of him, and that was not helpful. On one occasion, I was Fourth Official to Matt Messias at Derby versus Coventry. Matt was very young and trying out for the Premier League. During the game I tried to encourage him with thumbs-up gestures and positive body language. But one of the Coventry coaches was less impressed than I was and filled in a sub card and handed it to me. It said, 'Player off: Messias. Player on: Poll'.

When I was refereeing matches, I tried to make good use of the Fourth Official. He changed in the ref's room with me and the assistants, attended all the pre-match briefings, got miked up and so on, and was part of the refereeing team. But I didn't have him warming up with me and the two assistants. That was partly because there was no point and partly because he was more use staying in the ref's room. That was where the phone would ring if anyone wanted to contact me about something, like delaying the kick-off because of trouble outside the ground. That was also where he could deal with late administrative stuff, like changes to the team-sheets if a player was injured during the warm-up.

When the time came for me to brief my team, my instructions to the Fourth Official would be, 'Don't be too pedantic. Don't be too picky. But make sure the managers let the assistant on their side of the pitch get on with his duties without any hassle.'

For me, that was and is the prime value of a Fourth Official: he takes the stick from angry managers instead of the assistant referee, who would otherwise get it in the ear as the nearest available man in black (or green, or yellow).

For matches abroad, I had a big say in who was the Fourth Official. The procedure was that UEFA or FIFA would inform the English FA that I had been appointed for such and such a match, and then the FA would appoint the two assistants and the Fourth Official. The FA knew that we would be away together for three days, and that it would not be a good idea to send a team of officials who didn't get on with each other. The FA knew who I was friendly with and, more importantly, whose company I did not enjoy. In case they were in any doubt, I blackballed a couple by saying, 'don't put them on trips with me'.

You can't only take your mates though. Going abroad as a Fourth Official is a chance to learn and get experience, so when I was a senior ref I was sometimes asked to take someone on his way up.

On the whole though, I think the Fourth Official function is fraught with difficulties – not least in circumstances such as the Zidane scenario. The choice for Luis Medina Cantalejo in Berlin at the World Cup Final might have been to ignore the letter of the law or ignore a head-butt. That cannot be right.

And consider, once again, the 'phantom goal' awarded to Reading at Watford (on 20 September 2008). There was no television monitor in the technical areas that day. The rules had been changed at the start of the season for the Premier League and Football League to stop managers seeing mistakes by referees and immediately confronting them about them.

Watford manager Aidy Boothroyd, standing next to the Fourth Official, saw with his own eyes that the ball had gone nowhere near the goal. The Fourth Official decided, properly according to the Laws, not to say anything to referee Stuart Attwell. Later in the game, however, Boothroyd, who was understandably still incensed about the 'goal', said something rude about a throw-in decision and the Fourth Official said he would report him. Boothroyd replied, 'Oh, you couldn't tell a ref about a goal that wasn't, but you can tell the ref about that all right, can't you?' The Fourth Official did report Boothroyd, who was sent to the stand by the ref.

MORE RED CARDS FOR ZIDANE

AFTER his sending off, but before the end of extra-time and before the penalties were taken, there was an announcement over the public address system at the stadium which summed up the paradoxical Zinedine Zidane. It was announced that he had won the Golden Ball award for the World Cup's best player. The award was determined by a vote of journalists at the Final. The votes were collected at half-time, and by the time the count had been conducted, Zidane was back in the dressing room in disgrace and those same journalists were compiling reports which condemned him for resorting to violence. That conflict, between celebrating Zidane's skills and castigating him for savagery, was a constant throughout his career.

If we start to play the role of amateur psychologists, there is a danger we will make assumptions that are not accurate. But it must be right that Zidane's childhood helped shape the man he became, so we have to record that he was the youngest of five children born to immigrant parents in a housing project in a rough part of Marseille. Football, played beautifully, was his escape route from that tough start, but did he take some of the instincts of a street fighter with him?

Vinnie Jones, now known for acting as a 'baddie' in films, really was a baddie when I was refereeing. He probably had the reputation as the hardest player of my era and was sent off 13 times. Zidane was sent off a total of 14 times.

The Scottish referee Stuart Dougal set some kind of record by sending off both Zidane and the Dutchman Edgar Davids in the same Juventus Champions League match in 2000. It is not every ref who red cards two of the best players of the world in the same evening. Zidane's sending off was for a retaliatory head-butt. At least two of the Frenchman's other dismissals were also for head-butts. One was for stamping on an opponent. So perhaps we should not have been so shocked that he erupted with fury in the World Cup Final. In some ways, it was an entirely appropriate way for his career to end because it was in keeping with what had gone before.

But this complicated man, who could be so violent towards opponents, could bring a football under control with the deftest, gentle touch and was capable of great artistry on the football pitch. Bixente Lizarazu, who played with him for Bordeaux and France, said, 'When we didn't know what to do, we just gave the ball to Zizou and he worked something out.'

From the back streets of Marseille came the most expensive player in the world. He won league titles in Italy and Spain. He won the World Cup and the European Championship. He was FIFA's world player of the year three times. His two goals as France won in 1998, together with his penalty in 2006, mean that he scored in two World Cup Finals. Yet his last act as a pro was to head-butt an opponent.

3

A BIG HAND FOR MARADONA

THE MATCH

Like Zinedine Zidane, Diego Armando Maradona grew up in a humble family and went on to become the pre-eminent player of his generation. Some will tell you that Maradona was the greatest of all time. But, as with Zidane, it is impossible to assess the Argentine without factoring in an offence committed at a World Cup – and I am an England fan, so you know where I stand. As far as I am concerned, the notorious 'Hand of God' goal against England during the 1986 World Cup disqualifies Maradona from inclusion alongside Pele and Johan Cruyff in the very top bracket of the best ever to have played the game. And, from a modern perspective, the way Maradona cheated that day asks some questions for referees and for the game itself. So let's get in the time machine again. Set the dial for 1986.

In Mexico, the 13th staging of the World Cup finals involved three teams from the United Kingdom. Scotland were eliminated at the group stage, losing to Denmark and West Germany and gleaning their single point from a goalless game against Uruguay. Their only goal in three matches was scored by Gordon Strachan. Northern Ireland were also knocked out with just one point, although their group included Brazil and Spain, and they did finish above Algeria.

England, meanwhile, stuttered along unconvincingly until, on 11 June, a Gary Lineker hat-trick gave them victory against Poland. That made them group runners-up behind Morocco and saw them through to the first knock-out stage, the 'round of 16'. England did not appear to be in the sort of form to worry anyone, least of all Argentina, who breezed through their group with two wins and a draw, and for whom Maradona was living up to his pre-tournament billing as a major talent.

But England were getting into their stride at the right time and two more goals from Lineker and one from Peter Beardsley saw them ease past Paraguay 3–0 (in Mexico City on 18 June) to set up a quarter-final against Argentina, 1–0 winners against Uruguay. The three other quarter-finals all went to penalties. The attendance for England's quarter-final in the Aztec Stadium in Mexico City (on 22 June) was an astonishing 115,000. The fateful moment came after 51 scoreless minutes.

England had just dealt with one attack and most players were still in our half. Maradona, dropping deep, took possession about 40 yards from our goal, about ten metres in from our right touchline, and started motoring forwards. Two rows of England players were stationed in front of him and Glenn Hoddle stepped forward from the ranks to close him down. The little Argentine simply swayed away to his right and left the future England coach stranded. As Barry Davies said on the BBC television commentary, with a tone of mounting concern, 'Maradona just walked away from Hoddle.'

Peter Reid, playing left midfield, ran back and across but the Argentine's acceleration had carried him away before Reid got there. Three defenders came out from the edge of the penalty area to try to deal with the obvious and increasing threat but they too were left marooned out of position as Maradona, now equidistant between the two sidelines, used his left foot to stab the ball to his right towards a team-mate, Jorge Valdano, who was standing inside the D of the penalty area, with his back to goal.

Valdano's attempt to control the pass sent the ball spiralling upwards. The player marking him, Steve Hodge, stuck up his left leg and miskicked the ball higher into the air and back towards his own goalkeeper, Peter Shilton. Maradona had continued his run, hoping for a one-two with Valdano. Shilton came out to punch away Hodge's miscued attempted clearance. Maradona arrived at the same time as the ball. Up went Maradona. Up went Maradona's left arm. Cue pandemonium.

Maradona used his clenched hand to flip the ball up and over Shilton's attempted punch and into the goal. Maradona immediately started celebrating but, at first, none of his team-mates joined in. So he waved them towards him. Shilton pointed to his own arm, in a gesture that the watching world knew meant, 'Handball!' The goal-keeper sprinted out to the referee to protest and other England play-ers joined him. But the ref had already signalled a goal and the goal stood.

Four minutes later, Maradona scored a second goal, one of the best ever seen in a major match. Watching it again now, you wonder whether you're playing the clip in fast mode. Maradona had his back to our goal when he gained possession inside his own half but a trail of flailing defenders was left like flotsam in his wake as he span around and just kept running before beating Shilton legitimately. Lineker collected a goal for England ten minutes before the end, his sixth of the tournament. But Argentina won 2–1. They beat Belgium in the semi-final, and then, in front of another 115,000 crowd at the Aztec (on 29 June), Argentina beat West Germany 3–2 in the Final. Maradona was carried around the pitch shoulder high, holding the trophy aloft. Like Zidane 20 years later, he was voted the tournament's best player despite his moment of infamy in the match against England.

THE ISSUES

Immediately after the quarter-final against England, Maradona was interviewed by media representatives from around the world. He was asked, 'Wasn't your first goal handball?' He replied that it was *un poco con la cabeza de Maradona y otro poco con la mano de Dios* (a little with the head of Maradona and another little with the hand of God).

Hand of God. The phrase has echoed down the years, but it was an ambiguous answer; certainly not an admission. The admission came many years later. In his autobiography, published in 2002, Maradona said, 'It was the hand of Diego and it felt a little like pick-pocketing the English.' Yet, although he has come clean about what happened, he has remained ambivalent about the act, appearing apologetic in some interviews given to English media but steadfastly defiant when talking for Argentine audiences about the incident.

There is no ambivalence in Argentina. *La Mano de Dios* came only four years after Argentina had been at war with Britain in the Falklands and Maradona's compatriots were overjoyed by the football victory after defeat in battle. Argentina worships Maradona, not despite the fact that he scored with his hand against England, but because of it.

Scottish football fans revere Maradona for exactly the same reason: he put one over England. When Maradona became coach to the Argentine national team, his first game in charge (on 21 November 2008) was at Hampden Park against Scotland. *The Daily Record* newspaper created a logo for all their extensive coverage of the fixture. It read, 'A big hand for Diego'. The newspaper also reported a terrace song. Gleefully sung to the tune of the Hokey Cokey, it went, 'You put your left hand in and you shake it all about. You do the hokey-cokey and you score a goal, that's what it's all about. Oh-ohh, Diego Maradona!'

So, to many people, what Maradona did was not only acceptable, it was admirable. But before English readers get too censorious, let's consider this: should an Englishman have up-ended Maradona in 1986 when he was homing in on our penalty area for his second goal? Bobby Robson, who was England's manager that day in 1986, wrote in 2008 that if Bryan Robson had been fit to play against Argentina he would have stopped Maradona 'one way or another'. Would we have complained? I doubt it very much.

Yet, surely, deliberately fouling an opponent is a form of cheating. Or is it? For me, the Hand of God incident raises two intriguing questions: what constitutes cheating in football, and when is cheating acceptable on the field of play? You might think it is easy to answer both questions. You might believe that any deliberate act that is outside the laws of the game is cheating and that it is never acceptable. Yet when I was refereeing I was constantly reminded that the line between what is legal and illicit is often blurred.

For instance, if a player goes down without being tripped or kicked, he's cheating, isn't he? Not necessarily. If he jumps out of the way of a bad challenge, he is behaving sensibly and properly. So when a player goes down without there having been any contact, a ref has to decide whether he is preserving his own shins or just diving. One high-profile incident like that occurred on 19 August 2006 at Bramall Lane. Liverpool's Steven Gerrard hit the deck in the penalty area although there had been no contact from Sheffield United's Chris Morgan. Rob Styles, the referee, awarded a penalty and explained later that, in his opinion, Morgan had intended to foul Gerrard, who had skipped out of the way and fallen to the floor. Styles received lots of stick, predictably, from writers and broadcasters for talking about 'intent'. Equally predictably, Neil Warnock, who was the Sheffield United manager, was particularly scathing about the very idea of a match official trying to guess Morgan's intentions. He was highly critical of Styles. No change there then. But Law Twelve says that it is a foul if someone trips or attempts to trip an opponent. That law required Styles to decide what Morgan was trying to do. The ref was right and Warnock was wrong. No change there, either.

Another example came at Ewood Park on 9 November 2008 when Chelsea's Nicolas Anelka chased a poor back-pass into the Blackburn Rovers' penalty area. Goalkeeper Paul Robinson came out and, in trying to evade the challenge, Anelka lost his balance. That time, the ref, Chris Foy, did not award a penalty. I am not sure he was right, but I am sure it is always an extremely difficult judgement call.

Now, what about when a player feels the merest touch of an opponent's boot against his shin and tumbles to the ground? Does he have a right to make sure everyone realizes that he has been fouled, however slightly? I can tell you that there were many occasions, when I was refereeing, when a player stayed upright after getting his shin tapped and I said to myself, under my breath, 'If you'd gone down there, I'd have given a penalty.' But I didn't give anything, because there would have been no credibility in penalizing the defender for such a slight touch with the attacker still on his feet. So, do you blame strikers for flinging themselves to the floor if they feel contact in the penalty area? I don't.

To complicate matters further, there are times when an attacker effectively causes the foul against him – but it is still a foul. One example featured Thierry Henry when he was playing for France against England. It was on 17 June 2004 in the European Championships in Portugal. Henry was chasing the ball into the English penalty area and our goalkeeper, David James, was rushing out of his goal to get to the ball first. I believe that Henry calculated that, if he could arrive fractionally before James and tip the ball away with his toe, then the goalkeeper's momentum would bring about a foul. That is exactly what happened. Henry toe-ended the ball, and James, who was already diving to either block a shot or get his hands on the ball, inadvertently clattered into the French striker and knocked away his legs. Quite correctly, a penalty was awarded, Zidane scored it and France won 2–1. Henry's only intention as he raced forward had been to invite the foul. But it was still a foul – and I don't imagine anyone would consider what Henry did was cheating. So I hope you can see that the whole question of going down in the penalty area is not at all straightforward.

Now put yourself in the boots of a defender. An opponent beats you with speed or sleight of foot and, although you go for the ball, you kick his leg instead. It's a foul. Simple. But if the player beats you fairly and squarely and, after he has gone past you, you scythe him down to stop him getting away, it's a foul again, but it is a worse type of foul. We can all agree on that, I hope. So, what if, once the opponent has beaten you with the ball, you grab his shirt from behind and stop him? Is that better or worse than scything him down? In one sense, the shirt-grabbing is less heinous than hacking someone down. Knocking over an opponent could do serious damage. Shirt-grabbing usually does not endanger anyone's health. But some would argue that grabbing a shirt is more devious and less part of football.

So now let's go back to Maradona. His handball against England did not put anyone in danger of injury but it was duplicitous. So, if someone had fouled him deliberately as he closed in on his second goal, would that have been better or worse than his handball? Would it have been acceptable?

I have a few more scenarios to consider. Did any Englishman complain when Lineker went down extremely easily in the penalty area (on 1 July 1990) in a World Cup quarter-final against Cameroon? Was there a single English murmur of disquiet on 7 June 2002 when Michael Owen crumpled to the floor to win a penalty against Argentina in the World Cup? When David Beckham converted the penalty, we all went wild. Did any of us question Owen's willingness to go down? What about when Peter Crouch tugged the dreadlocks of Brent Sancho to climb above him and head England's goal against Trinidad and Tobago on 10 June 2006 in the World Cup?

One more question. This one goes to me as well as to you. If Wayne Rooney handles the ball to score a goal in a World Cup quarter-final, would we be as critical of him as we have been of Maradona?

Interestingly, an Englishman did 'score' with his hand in a big match. Paul Scholes tried it for Manchester United against Zenit St Petersburg in the European Super Cup Final on 28 August 2008. Danish referee Claus Bo Larsen spotted it and cautioned him. It was his second yellow card and so he was sent off. But if Scholes had got away with it, what would he have said afterwards? What would *we* have said?

Do you still think that the issue of cheating is straightforward and clear-cut?

Maradona's Hand of God goal raises a refereeing question as well. How on earth did the match officials miss the handball? The referee was a Tunisian, Ali Bennaceur. When newspapers hark back to that day, many state categorically that the quarter-final was Bennaceur's first and last match as a World Cup referee. That is nonsense. Not even FIFA would expect a man to go straight into such a highly pressurized situation. He refereed an earlier match (in England's group, as it happens) between Portugal and Poland. He also ran the line in a couple of matches before the quarter-final. However, because of his horrific mistake in permitting the Hand of God goal, the quarter-final was certainly his last World Cup match.

THE REF'S DECISION

The role of the linesman was crucial that day in 1986 – or rather, the lack of action by the linesman, Bogdan Dotchev, from Bulgaria. He was in the standard position, level with the second-last defender. There was no question of offside, and no 'ball in and out of play' to worry about. He was looking across at the incident, with an unimpaired view. Shilton is six feet, one inch tall and had his arms up to punch the ball. Maradona is five feet five. To 'score' the Argentine had to have his own hand several inches above his head. After the incident, Maradona looked immediately towards the linesman, presumably fearing that he had seen the handball. So why on earth didn't Dotchev spot it?

Well, here is a stunning and appalling revelation. He claimed that he did. Dotchev said he saw the handball but did not flag. It took him more than two decades to make that statement, but it is a breathtaking admission. In an interview in January 2007, Dotchev argued that, once the referee had signalled a goal, he could not intervene. His exact words were, 'With the ref having said the goal was valid, I couldn't have waved my flag and told him the goal wasn't good – the rules were different back then.'

No, they were not. The rules – Laws actually, Bogdan – certainly did not prevent a linesman from signalling for an infringement. I don't doubt that FIFA's general instructions to linesmen included telling them to allow the refs to referee. I imagine as well that on the day of the quarter-final referee Ali Bennaceur would have told the two linesmen – Dotchev and Berny Ulloa Morera from Costa Rica –

to let him make the key decisions. But nothing in the instructions or the Laws of the Game then or now absolves the linesman of responsibility. If he saw a handball such as Maradona's, and the referee did not see it, he had a duty to signal.

Note that in 1986 there was no attempt to use officials with a common language. That came later, but it was not the issue. Whatever language you speak, if you spot a handball, you flag for it. It is much more significant that this was before specialist assistant referees were introduced at World Cups. Referees shared the task of running the line. You need to know, as well, that referees are competitive and can be resentful when others get the appointments they expected or desired. With that background, read some more of the comments made by Dotchev about that day in 1986. He said, 'European refs take charge of at least one or two important games per month and are used to big-match pressure. What is there for Bennaceur to referee in the desert where there is nothing but camels?'

That is a deeply unpleasant remark. Yet behind it lie a couple of uncomfortable truths that persist to this day. One is that there are areas of the world where the football is less demanding to referee, yet referees from those areas are asked to officiate in World Cups. The second truth is that some officials allow small-minded resentment to fester and corrode their attitude.

There are only two sets of circumstances to explain Dotchev's inaction. One is that, despite his comments 21 years later, he actually missed Maradona's handball. Later, realizing what a dreadful omission that would have been, he came up with his story about not being able to overrule the ref. The other possible explanation is that he did see the handball, as he claimed, but did not tell the referee for some reason. Both sets of circumstances are equally unforgivable.

Let me deal now with what the ref should have done once the 'goal' had gone in. The reaction of the England players was manic and, in those circumstances, a referee's gut feeling should tell him that he's got something wrong. There were many occasions in my career when I just knew, from the response of players, that they were right and I was wrong. But, usually, I didn't change my mind. That was not me being pig-headed; that was me abiding by the principle that a referee can only give what he sees (or thinks he sees). If you start down the road of changing your mind when players challenge your decision, then you are undermining the whole basis on which football is refereed – which is that the ref makes an honest decision based on his view of events. I accept, however, that it is a very complex area of debate.

On 30 December 2008, when Aston Villa were playing at Hull in the Premier League, Villa's Ashley Young was defending a corner and jumped up on the goal-line with his fist above his head. After some hesitation, referee Steve Bennett initially awarded Hull a penalty but the Villa players went berserk and suddenly 'Benno' ran over to his assistant, Andy Halliday. The two officials had a discussion and then Bennett made it clear that he had changed his mind. It wasn't a penalty. He signalled a goal-kick instead. He is normally the least equivocal referee you could find, far less likely to change his mind than I was – and I very, very seldom changed it. This time, however, Bennett altered his decision. TV replays showed that the ball had struck the crossbar, and not Young's fist.

So, eventually, Benno had arrived at the decision which was correct. But although it was right for the match, I think it was wrong for the Game.

If referees change their minds because of the reaction of players, then they are encouraging players to react. Yet referees want the authorities to prevent hounding by big groups of players every time there is a contentious decision. The most notorious example of a referee being mobbed was on 29 January 2000 when Andy D'Urso was forced to keep stepping backwards as a pack of Manchester United men confronted him.

In my own career, I felt badly let down when I complained about Chelsea players haranguing me when I was in charge of their match against Tottenham at White Hart Lane on 5 November 2006. The FA decided that I did not look intimidated, and so did not charge Chelsea with trying to intimidate me. I felt strongly that the FA had missed the point. The behaviour of the Chelsea players was the issue, not how I responded, and the FA should never do anything that encourages players to swarm around referees trying to get them to change their decisions. Nor should referees themselves, and so, generally speaking, officials should not change their minds when confronted by complaining players.

However, it is perfectly correct for a ref to factor the reaction of players into his decision-making. That is subtly different and the difference is important.

So, let's step into the boots of referee Bennaceur for that World Cup match. Let's remember that there is a huge crowd and he is under intense pressure – more than he has ever experienced. The first thing to say is that his positioning should have been better. He should have put himself somewhere so that he could see what happened, and he should have spotted Maradona's handball.

Even if he did not see it, I would have expected the ref to think, instinctively, that there was something wrong because a short player had somehow managed to make contact with the ball above a tall goalkeeper. I would have expected the ref to wonder, 'How did that happen?' In the modern era, the referee would then say into his lip microphone, 'Are you all happy with that goal?' The question would be addressed mainly to the assistant referee at the end at which the goal was scored, but also to the other one – who is referred to in refereeing circles as 'the dead end assistant'.

My instructions to my assistants used to include what to do in circumstances like Maradona's Hand of God 'goal'. I used to say, 'When the ball goes into the net, if you have seen an offence (offside, handball, anything), then you must flag. If you are not sure what happened, but think something is not right, don't flag. Hold your ground and look at me, as if to say, "I'm not happy here Pollie. Something is wrong." If I have the same feeling, I will probably run over to you and, between us, we can sort it out.'

When I was among the referees at the 2002 World Cup, FIFA's guidance to us was that we should trust our gut instincts. They said that was why we had been selected: because we had a feel for the game. In circumstances like Maradona's handball, that instruction would encourage me to think that there was something wrong.

Part of the evidence would be the reaction of England's players. That is not the same as saying that, after awarding the goal, the ref should have changed his mind *because* of the reaction of Shilton and the other England players. I don't think he should have. But, having sensed that something was wrong with the goal, the way Maradona looked at the linesman, the instinctive reluctance of his team-mates to celebrate immediately and the outrage of the England men should all have added to the referee's unease.

I am not saying that the ref should consult the assistant because of the pressure applied by players from the team that has conceded a 'goal'. Definitely not. I am saying that the suspicion that something is not right comes first, then the discussion with the assistant – and then, like a detective considering all the available evidence, the ref is correct to take into account the behaviour of players from both teams.

However, the ref might still have had to award the goal. If I had refereed the Hand of God match, and not seen Maradona's handball, I like to think that I would have been sufficiently suspicious because of Maradona's height to ask the linesman what he had seen. But if the linesman had said, 'I didn't see anything wrong', then I would have awarded the goal. I had not seen anything that would give me reason to disallow it. That is the only honest way to referee a foot-ball match.

So although Bennaceur got a big decision wrong, and although England suffered, it was probably beneficial for the Game. It reminded everyone that referees sometimes make human errors and can only give what they see.

Now let's return to the conundrum of what constitutes cheating. That is one question I can't answer in this book, because I can't answer it categorically in my own mind. It comes down to what you believe about football, what you feel, and so everyone will have his or her own idea about what is an 'honest' foul and what is cheating. I just know that, when I was refereeing, it was deception that really annoyed me. So, although much of South America, all of Scotland and some of you will disagree, I do have an opinion about Maradona's Hand of God deception. Was it better or worse than hacking someone down? I think it was worse.

My final conclusion to be drawn from *la Mano de Dios* is this: some players are willing and prepared to cheat. You might think that is obvious and not at all profound but it is at the core of the continuous debate about refereeing standards, respecting officials and so on.

Yes, referee Bennaceur should have spotted the handball. Yes, linesman Dotchev should have signalled. But the chain of events at the Aztec Stadium in 1986 began when a footballer flagrantly flouted the Laws and went against the spirit of the Game.

When someone commits an offence on a football field there are too many people who say, 'Well, it is up to the referee to spot it.' As we shall see, that seems to be Lineker's attitude. I certainly accept that referees have got to strive to improve their detection of cheating and other types of offences. But let's not forget that it is the players who commit the offences.

The next time a referee is deceived by a dive, misled by some form of deception, or simply misses seeing an offence, it would be nice if the manager, players and supporters of the team who suffer that injustice remember that the 'crime' against them was committed by the footballer, not the referee.

WORLD CUP STATS: 1986

QUALIFICATION TOURNAMENT: Canada, Denmark and Iraq qualified for the first time. Canada won their final qualifying match against Honduras 2–1 in Newfoundland, with the Hondurans wearing woollen hats and gloves. Iraq played all their home matches in Kuwait because of the Iran–Iraq war. Scotland's qualification was marred by tragedy. On 10 September 1985, Scotland drew 1–1 with Wales at Ninian Park. The result was sufficient to secure qualification. But manager Jock Stein suffered a heart attack at the end of the game and died shortly afterwards in the stadium's medical room, aged 62.

FINALS: 31 May to 29 June. Twenty-four teams from five federations

HOSTS: Mexico

MASCOT: Pique (a jalapeño pepper, with a moustache and a sombrero)

FINAL: Argentina 3, West Germany 2

MATCHES PLAYED: 52

GOALS SCORED: 132

ATTENDANCE: 2,393,331

TOP SCORER: Gary Lineker (England, 6 goals)

BEST PLAYER: Diego Maradona (Argentina)

HOME NATIONS: England, managed by Bobby Robson, beaten in quarter-finals by Argentina. Scotland, managed by Alex Ferguson, eliminated with just one point from their three matches, a goalless draw with Uruguay. Northern Ireland, managed by Billy Bingham, reached the tournament as runners-up in England's qualifying group. In Mexico, Northern Ireland drew 1–1 with Algeria, then were beaten 2–1 by Spain and 3–0 by Brazil. Pat Jennings won his 119th and final international cap in goal for Northern Ireland against Brazil – on his 41st birthday.

TV 'REPLAYS' REVEAL TRUTHS

Years after he stopped playing, Maradona was given his own chat-show on Argentine television, called *La Noche del 10* (The Night of the 10). On one of those programmes, in 2005, he gave some more details of what happened in the game against England. He said the handball was not premeditated. It was 'something that just came out of me. It was a bit of mischief.' He added, 'I was waiting for my team-mates to embrace me and no one came. I told them, "Come hug me or the referee isn't going to allow it".'

One of his opponents in the England team, Lineker, also became a TV host, of course. Lineker filmed an interview with Maradona for the BBC before the 2006 World Cup. The two former players sat by the side of a swimming pool in Argentina and discussed the events in Mexico 20 years earlier. Lineker said that Maradona's second goal was probably the only time he had ever come close to applauding an opponent during a match. Maradona responded just as graciously, saying that probably he would not have been permitted to score that second, legitimate goal against a country other than England. Anyone else would have fouled him. He said, 'The English player is a lot more noble, a lot more honest on the pitch.'

That might be an example of playing to his audience, and I'm not sure anyone could have fouled Maradona during his run for the second goal. When he played against Scotland on one occasion, some of the Scottish players said they'd tried to foul him but had just bounced off him because he was so strong and had such good balance and a low centre of gravity.

But Maradona's praise for the noble English echoes my own internal debate about what constitutes cheating and what is acceptable, and, in that interview with Lineker, Maradona not only said that Englishmen were too decent to foul him but also that the South American attitude to some forms of cheating is different to ours. He said, 'It was my hand (but) no, I don't think it was cheat-ing. Cunning, cheekiness, craftiness, but not cheating. Maybe we have more of it in South America than in Europe. I don't mean any disrespect to England fans but this is something that happens. I had scored goals before in Argentina with my hand. I couldn't reach it and Shilton was already there. I couldn't head it, so I did it like that.'

His comment about the attitude in South America is a generalization, of course, but there is some truth in it. There are some areas of the world where, in my experience, some people do regard some forms of duplicitous behaviour on a sports field as ingenious rather than wrong. In media interviews before the Scotland game in 2008, Maradona was asked yet again about the Hand of God goal. He said that he did not see how the English could complain about 1986 because we had won the World Cup in 1966 with a goal 'when the ball did not cross the line'. The difference – between cheating in 1986 and accepting the decision of a linesman 20 years earlier – was lost on him, apparently.

One other comment in Lineker's 2006 interview with Maradona struck a raw nerve with me. During their poolside chat, Lineker said, 'Personally I blame the referee and the linesman, not you (for the Hand of God goal).' Both men laughed, but there are plenty of people who say the same sort of thing perfectly seriously. That is like blaming the police for crime.

BUTCHER'S GRUDGE

In many ways it is extraordinary that Maradona became Argentina's national coach. He is not exactly an ideal role model. He did play in four World Cups, but some of you might remember his wide-eyed stare and maniacal scream at the cameras after one goal in the 1994 finals in the USA. He did not look like a well man and soon afterwards was sent home in disgrace for using ephedrine. He had already served a 15-month suspension for taking cocaine and, when he finally retired from playing, drug abuse contributed to serious health issues. He became obscenely overweight and his behaviour grew erratic. I suppose, though, that he deserves some credit for pulling his life together eventually.

Scotland's assistant manager for the Hampden international against Maradona's Argentina in 2008 was Terry Butcher. Twenty-two years earlier he had been one of the England players lined up against Maradona, and so he pointedly refused to have anything to do with him before the Hampden game. Butcher still felt cheated. He believed the 1986 team, which included some very good players, might well have gone on to win the World Cup if they had beaten Argentina. He said he would not shake Maradona's hand because it was the so-called Hand of God. Actually, the offending hand was Maradona's left and not his right.

NOT SO SPLENDID ISOLATION

I don't need a time machine to take me back to 1986. I can remember one event that year with absolute clarity – the moment George Courtney welcomed me to the top group of match officials.

It was the year that I became a Football League linesman. I went to the summer conference for Football League officials for the first time, in Harrogate. On the first evening there was a formal reception and as I walked into the auditorium the first person to say hello was the great George Courtney.

Six years earlier, when he was in charge of the FA Cup Final (between West Ham and Arsenal), I went to the banquet which was held on the eve of the Final each year by the London Society of Referees. George was guest of honour. I went to gawp at him.

He worked as a primary school head teacher in his native Spennymoor, County Durham, and was the dominant figure of English refereeing of the 1980s, although towards the end of that decade, Keith Hackett (who went on to be my boss at the Select Group) shared the top billing.

George completed the hat-trick of big Wembley fixtures – the FA Cup Final, the Charity Shield and the League Cup Final – but then, in an unprecedented move, he was given a second League Cup Final. He was on FIFA's international list for 14 years, and refereed at the 1984 European Championships and the World Cups of 1986 and 1990.

At the 1986 World Cup, he took charge of Mexico's group match against Paraguay, which is an indication of his standing, because FIFA would have wanted someone in whom they had the utmost trust to referee the host nation at the Aztec Stadium. Then, after the semi-finals, George refereed the third-place match, between France and Belgium – the furthest any English referee had reached since the incomparable Jack Taylor controlled the 1974 Final, and unequalled since.

It was not long after flying home from the 1986 World Cup that George went to that conference in Harrogate. So for me to meet him was as big a deal as it would be for my young son, Harry, to meet David Beckham. Yet George looked out for me, the youngest ever Football League linesman at that stage, and said some words of welcome and encouragement. I was knocked out by that. How fantastic. It was the sort of thing that top referees did then, but don't get the opportunity to do now.

These days the Select Group are creamed off and separated from the blokes and women lower down the refereeing ladder. There are benefits from training and preparing for matches together, and scrutinizing each other's performances in the Premier League, but by isolating the Select Group from the rest, something worthwhile has been lost.

YELLOW CARD FOR MESSI

FROM the moment he helped Argentina win the World Youth Championships in 2005 and was voted the tournament's best player, Lionel Messi has attracted comparisons with Maradona. And, for the 2006 World Cup, Messi had a highly controversial tribute to Maradona stitched into the design

of his personalized football boots. The words 'La Mano de Dios 86' were embroidered on the side. That confirmed again that, far from being ashamed of the Hand of God goal, some Argentines revelled in its memory.

On 18 April 2007 Messi emulated Maradona's wonderful, legitimate second goal against England in the 1986 World Cup. Playing for Barcelona against Getafe in the semi-final of the Spanish Cup, Messi ran more than half the length of the pitch and carried the ball past five opponents before scoring.

Then, two months later on 10 June, Messi scored his own version of Maradona's Hand of God goal. This time, Barcelona's opponents were their city rivals, Espanol. Barcelona were losing 1–0 when Gianluca Zambrotta crossed and Messi punched it in. I would absolve the referee and his assistant from blame because, unlike Maradona (who had his fist high above his head), Messi had his hand beside his head, on the blind side of the assistant.

Had the referee or his assistant seen the handball, then Messi should have been cautioned for flouting the Law. And those in Argentina, Spain and elsewhere who chuckled when they read about what Messi had sewn on his boots in 2006 might like to reflect about the attitude those words reflected.

THE MYTHS OF HANDBALL

Handball is the best illustration of one of the facts about football – which is that although it is the world's most popular game, most people do not know its laws.

You hear people talk about 'ball to hand' or 'hand to ball' as if those phrases are enshrined in holy writ. Then there is the almost unanimous belief that if a player deliberately handles the ball, he must be booked. If a goalkeeper handles the ball outside his area, people say he should be sent off.

That is all rubbish.

So let's quash all the myths. Let's look at what the Law says. Handball is dealt with in Law Twelve, which lists 'fouls and misconduct'. The law specifies ten offences which warrant a direct free-kick or penalty. One of them is when a player 'handles the ball deliberately'. So the offence of handball is defined in four words: 'handles the ball deliberately'. That's it.

Every time the ball makes contact with a player's hand or arm you will hear those associated with the other team call, 'Handball!' Players yell it, managers bellow it, spectators scream it, mums and dads watching a Sunday morning seven-a-side for kids shout it. If the ref ignores the clamour, there is disbelief all round. Yet, often the ref is entirely right because any unintentional handling is OK. If the referee decides the contact was accidental, then it is not an offence, regardless of where it takes place and regardless of the consequences.

That means that another phrase you hear from time to time – "accidental handball" – is rubbish. As far as the Law is concerned, if it is accidental, it's not handball. If it's handball, it can't have been accidental.

There is nothing at all in the Law about 'hand to ball' or 'ball to hand.' If a player is moving his arm naturally and it accidentally strikes the ball, it's not an offence (although it might be 'hand to ball'). If a player intentionally puts his arm into the line of flight of the ball, and there is contact, then it is an offence (although it is 'ball to hand'). The Law simply says it is an offence if he 'handles the ball deliberately'.

Handball is not mentioned at all in the list of seven offences which must be punished with a yellow card, so that is another fallacy. Normally, a referee who knows and understands the Laws will merely punish handball with a free-kick or a penalty, as he would if the infringement was a simple foul. If the handball is particularly cynical, then the ref might caution the player for 'unsporting behaviour' as he would for a cynical foul. The only time handball warrants a red card is when the offence denies an obvious goal-scoring opportunity. Again, that is exactly the same as with a foul.

Handball is always treated just like fouling. It is no worse and no better. It does not carry a mandatory caution. It does not involve special sanctions at all.

So the only occasion when a goalkeeper should be sent off for handling the ball outside his area is when he has done so deliberately and has denied an obvious goal-scoring opportunity. In those circumstances, he is punished exactly as you would punish a defender who did the same thing.

I hope that is clearer now. What baffles, angers and frustrates me is that, despite the clarity of the Law, people sometimes don't believe referees when they tell them the plain truth. I've been in many situations when someone has said, 'That should have been a yellow card. It was deliberate handball.' When I say, 'That's not the Law', they say, 'Yes it is!' They don't ever bother to read the Laws themselves, but they are convinced they know them.

The next time you are at a match or in a pub watching a game and some know-all talks the usual nonsense about handball, you can tell him he's wrong. But he won't believe you.

 THE PURPOSE OF HANDBALL

THE wording of the handball law specifically raises the question of intent. If you kick or trip your opponent, even accidentally, it is a foul. But with handball, the referee always has to decide whether you committed the offence on purpose. So it is the most difficult law to apply accurately and consistently.

A referee should consider the speed at which the ball is travelling and the distance it travels before it hits (or is handled by) a player. I think a ref should consider the conditions as well. When the ground is bone hard, the ball is more likely to bounce up unexpectedly high, for example.

It is often a very difficult decision. Let's think about a specific example. In the opening match of Euro 96 (on 8 June), England played Switzerland at Wembley and were winning 1–0 with an Alan Shearer goal when Stuart Pearce jumped into a challenge. The ball struck one of his arms from very close range, a penalty was awarded and the Swiss got a draw. The English media was outraged but I don't think Pearce's hands were in a natural position. He was 'making himself big' to block the ball. He was not saying, 'I will handle it' but he was making a deliberate movement which led to the ball striking his arm. I think the referee – Manuel Diaz Vega of Spain – was correct.

Let's consider a different example. In the 2008/09 season, during Arsenal's home game against Manchester United (on 8 November 2008), the ball was fizzed in from United's right wing and Arsenal defender Gael Clichy made a movement of his arm just as the ball struck it. What sometimes happens in those circumstances is that a player realizes that the ball is heading at him and frantically tries to get his arm out of the way. There is not enough time to do so, and the movement looks as if he has tried to control the ball with his arm. In the Clichy case, United players all claimed handball. Referee Howard Webb waved away their appeals. I suspect that a panel of 12 neutral people looking at the incident in slow motion from a variety of angles would find it impossible to agree a unanimous verdict about whether it was *deliberate* handball. With that much uncertainty, I say Howard could not give a penalty.

RED CARD FOR OUR FA

TO help international referees in Europe, UEFA produce a booklet each year summarizing the guidance given during development programmes. My most recent copy is quite useful when thinking about handball. It says that, generally, if a player stops a promising attack by deliberately handling, he should be cautioned. If he prevents a goal being scored by deliberately handling he should be sent off. Otherwise, it reminds us, the only necessary punishment is a free-kick or penalty.

The booklet is small enough to slip into a jacket pocket (or a handbag). Our FA should pay for a copy to be sent to every registered referee in this country. Why don't they?

RED CARD FOR THE DIVERS

THE core message of this chapter is that it is players who cheat, so don't blame referees for events that sometimes ensue from that cheating. And that is particularly true of diving – or simulation, as FIFA insist on calling it.

There are three types of simulation. The first is where there is no contact at all and yet a player just throws himself to the ground. The second is when the attacker does suffer some contact by the opponent but exaggerates the effect of the contact – in other words, he feels a tiny tap on his ankle, for instance, but goes down as if felled by a sniper's shot. Of all the players I refereed, I'd say that Andy Johnson was the master of the art of making sure everyone knew his leg had been touched by an opponent's boot. He is with Fulham at the time of writing, but he made a name for himself at Crystal Palace and then went to Everton. If he is tapped in the penalty area, down he goes. I don't regard that as diving – but opposing players, managers and supporters often have a very different opinion.

The third type of simulation is when the diver initiates the contact, by dragging his trailing leg against the outstretched leg of the opponent, for instance, and then goes down as if fouled. That is a skill which is definitely practised by some players – and I do mean practised. They are so adept at it that they must teach themselves during training sessions.

Let's not kid ourselves that all this is new to our game, or something that we imported when our clubs started signing foreign players. It has always gone on, and Englishmen have been among those doing it. Rodney Marsh, the former England international who went on to become a controversial TV pundit, tells me he had a neat trick. He used to drag his own back foot into his front foot, trip himself up, and claim a foul!

But I do think modern players are getting better at it. It is certainly increasingly hard for referees to determine what is a foul and what is not. A particularly difficult area for refs is the question of players exaggerating the effect of contact on them. Sometimes, when there is a coming together of players, one player may believe he has been fouled and so will 'go to ground'. But the referee might conclude that the contact between the players was legal and so neither award a foul nor caution the player for simulation. You hear fans shout, 'It must be a foul or a card for diving!' But sometimes it is neither.

I hope I have established that the question of simulation is very difficult for referees. FIFA recognize that and, over the years, have said that if there is any contact at all between two players then the player who goes down should not be cautioned. Only in cases when it is blindingly obvious that an attacker has not been touched and yet has thrown himself to the ground should the ref get out his yellow card. FIFA have played safe, because they understand the difficulty of the judgements referees must make. It would be helpful if other football folk understood that as well.

So I go back to this thought: it is the players who make it hard for referees and if you think refereeing mistakes spoil the game, blame the players who set out to deceive them.

4

SCHUMACHER'S 'CRIME OF THE CENTURY'

THE MATCH

I can remember exactly where I was when I saw what French newspapers later called football's 'crime of the century'. I was in the bar of the Gordon Craig theatre and leisure centre in Stevenage, Hertfordshire. It was three weeks before my 19th birthday. It was the summer after my second season as a referee on parks pitches in Hertfordshire, and it was a training night for the North Herts Referees' Society. We used to have half an hour's fitness work, half an hour playing five-a-side football, and then we'd all pile into the bar and undo all the good work. On 8 July 1982 we adjourned to the bar with even more enthusiasm than usual. The World Cup in Spain had reached the semi-finals, West Germany were playing France, and there was a television in the bar. France had the brilliant Michel Platini as play-maker. West Germany were the reigning European champions. I remember it all so clearly because of the impact made on me by that 'crime of the century'. It made more of an impact on

French international Patrick Battiston. He lost consciousness and also mislaid a couple of teeth.

The match was in Seville. Pierre Littbarski gave the Germans the lead, but when Dominique Rocheteau was brought down by Bernd Förster in the area, Platini's penalty wrong-footed goalkeeper Harald Schumacher and equalized. At 1–1, the French sent on defender Battiston as a substitute and soon after his arrival on the pitch he ventured upfield and was sent scampering clear of the German defence by a Platini through ball. Schumacher came charging out, but was still only fractionally beyond his penalty spot when Battiston, just outside the area, began to lob the ball up and over the keeper with his left foot. Battiston's momentum carried him forward. Schumacher was still charging out. The goalkeeper leaped forwards and upwards, turned to his left in mid-air and collided with Battiston. The goalkeeper's right hip clouted the French player in the face. Battiston's head snapped backwards like a badly beaten prize-fighter and he was possibly unconscious before he hit the grass.

In the bar of the Gordon Craig theatre and leisure centre, and all over the world, it was like watching a car crash: a moment that made you shudder with horror but had a macabre fascination. Battiston received treatment where he lay. He was given oxygen. Platini said later that, for a moment, he believed Battiston was dead because he was so pale and looked so lifeless. Michel Hidalgo, the French coach, came onto the pitch and approached the Dutch referee, Charles Corver. But Hidalgo was more dismayed than angry, and produced a series of Gallic shrugs and sighs. The cause of his utter bewilderment was that the ref had indicated that he did not intend to punish Schumacher. He did not even give a free-kick. Battiston's lobbed shot had drifted wide and so, while the injured Frenchman was being partially revived and then carried from the field on a stretcher, goal-keeper Schumacher was placing the ball for a goal-kick, and that is how, eventually, play restarted.

The match went into extra-time but the additional period was only two minutes old when the French sweeper, Marius Tresor, volleyed his team ahead. Six minutes later, Alain Giresse put them 3–1 in front – much to the delight of most of the crowd, who had been booing and whistling every time Schumacher went near the ball and cheering every successful pass by the French. In Stevenage, we were all French fans for the night by then as well, but just before the end of the first half of extra-time, Karl-Heinz Rummenigge, the European Footballer of the Year, pulled a goal back for the Germans. In the second half of extra-time the French tried to curtail their adventurous nature and play with caution for the only time in the tournament. It did no good. Klaus Fischer scored with a marvellous overhead kick and it was 3–3.

Penalties. You know what happens when a match involving the Germans is decided by penalties. Both teams converted four of their first five spot-kicks and so it went to sudden death. Schumacher saved the sixth French penalty, taken by Maxime Bossis. Horst Hrubesch scored from the spot for West Germany. The French players wept openly. Somebody in Stevenage got a round in.

THE ISSUES

West Germany were beaten 3–1 by Italy in the final. France became champions of Europe two years later. Battiston also won the French Cup with Bordeaux and the league with Monaco. He played in three World Cups and eventually retired with 56 caps. He had a very good career and yet his name is mostly recalled for the terrible moment when he was pole-axed by Schumacher.

Five years later, Schumacher's autobiography was published. In it, he claimed that he had been 'going for the ball' and therefore his actions did not constitute a foul. At that time, fouls had to be intentional and so his defence was right in Law. But during the 1990s there were a number of changes to the wording of the Laws and the cumulative result means that now you can foul someone *un*intentionally, which will surprise many football fans.

In earlier decades, the game had been much slower and it was fairly easy to spot fouls, but as the speed of matches picked up so it became much harder to differentiate between deliberate trips and accidental clashes. It was also recognized that if a player is running with the ball, it doesn't matter to him whether he is tripped accidentally or intentionally. If an opponent clips his legs from behind, his progress is still stopped in a manner which is not a legal tackle. Similarly, if a player is kicked, it is not a lot of help to him to know that it was an accident. He has still been kicked.

Now Law Twelve (Fouls and Misconduct) says that it is a foul if a player commits any of seven offences in a way that is 'considered by the referee to be careless, reckless or using excessive force'. The seven are:

- **kicking or attempting to kick an opponent;**
- **tripping or attempting to trip an opponent;**
- **jumping at an opponent;**
- **charging an opponent;**
- **striking or attempting to strike an opponent;**
- **pushing an opponent;**
- **tackling an opponent.**

You can see that the Law just talks about tripping (or attempting to trip) and kicking (or attempting to kick). It doesn't say the trip or the kick has to be intentional. Referees are instructed that players have a 'duty of care' to each other. So if a defender is sprinting to catch up with an attacker, the defender has a duty of care not to run in such a way that his foot catches the back of the attacker's trailing leg, say, and causes him to stumble. If the defender does make the attacker fall, then, instead of exercising that duty of care he has been careless and, as the Law makes clear, that's a foul.

However, in 1982 Schumacher's alibi was correct about the Law. But very few people agreed with his version of events. From a refereeing point of view, the fact that the goalkeeper escaped punishment is almost inexplicable. He twisted his body in mid-air and that caused his bony hip to make the sickening contact with his opponent's head. I don't imagine that he intended to cause serious injury, but that mid-air change of body angle added to the threat caused by leaping straight at Battiston. It looked, at best, a dangerous, potentially calamitous challenge. Many commentators regard the incident as one of the worst fouls ever committed in a major match and one of the worst refereeing decisions not to send off Schumacher.

So why did the referee not even give a foul? Referee Corver was a salesman for Heineken. He was probably not the best referee in the world. But he was very well regarded. He refereed in the Dutch league, which was full of good players in the 1980s and certainly had plenty of competitive, pressurized matches. By the time he was selected for the 1982 World Cup, Corver had already been to the 1978 World Cup in Argentina and the 1980 European Championships in Italy. In Spain in 1982 he took charge of England's group match against Czechoslovakia before being given the semi-final, and although roundly criticized for his refusal to punish Schumacher, he continued his international career after the World Cup and later spent 16 years on the Dutch FA's disciplinary committee.

So how did someone that experienced and respected conclude that Schumacher had not fouled Battiston? The referee's positioning was good enough. When Platini made the pass that sent Battiston running through, Corver was fewer than ten metres away from Platini (probably too close, if anything). Platini was a few strides in from the right-hand French touchline and the ref was further infield, a little nearer to the German goal and standing facing the touchline. He was looking at Platini. When the pass was made, the ref turned to his left and started jogging towards the German goal. Perhaps he should have sprinted, because he was some distance away from the penalty area and there was the potential for a goal to be scored. But he had an unobscured view when the clash occurred. It was after the two players had collided that his behaviour seems shocking to modern eyes. He ambled up, apparently as unperturbed as Schumacher, as Battiston remained prone and motionless.

So perhaps he did not think Battiston was badly hurt. And if that is the case, perhaps he did not really see the collision. Perhaps he had glanced away momentarily to follow the flight of the ball. Who knows? What I do know is that I made a mistake myself which had some similarities.

At Selhurst Park on 3 January 2000, Wimbledon's Ben Thatcher and Sunderland's Nicky Summerbee confronted each other in a 50–50 challenge for the ball near the halfway line. Thatcher won, carried the ball away upfield, and I ran to keep up with play. It was a little while before my attention was drawn to Summerbee, who had been knocked over during the challenge and was still flat on the deck. I had no idea what had happened. Later, BBC's *Match of the Day* broadcast footage from a camera behind the goal Wimbledon had been defending. It was the only camera that captured the incident. It showed that, as Thatcher won the ball, he made a movement with his arm and caught Summerbee in the face. It looked like a wrestler's forearm smash. If I had seen it, I would have red-carded him. I didn't see it, however, because I was concentrating on the ball and on feet. I should have remained aware of their entire bodies.

Just over 15 months later, on 21 April 2001, at Upton Park, Leeds United's David Batty dispossessed West Ham's Joe Cole and Batty's forearm smashed into Cole's face. It was a very quick movement amid a flurry of limbs. The assistant referee on that side of the pitch missed it. I saw it – not because I was a genius, but because I had learned to watch the whole body instead of concentrating on feet and legs. I sent off Batty. The Leeds manager, David O'Leary, told *Match of the Day* that he did not know why I had shown his player the red card, but again the programme was able to find footage of exactly what had happened, and when they broadcast it, everyone knew why I had done it. My point is that I had to miss one before I learned to detect one.

Even so, over the years I did miss subsequent serious incidents. One of the worst challenges that I allowed to go unpunished was on 22 December 2002 at Anfield. Probably all of the 44,000 spectators thought Steven Gerrard's challenge on Gary Naysmith of Everton was a bad foul, even the Liverpool fans who adored Gerrard. One newspaper referred to the clash as 'blood-curdling'. But I didn't have a good view because a player ran across my line of sight at the critical moment, so I could not give a foul.

Two seasons later, on 2 October 2004 at Goodison Park, Tottenham captain Jamie Redknapp clattered into Everton's Tim Cahill with such ferocity that I showed Redknapp the yellow card. Cahill was quite badly hurt and had to be replaced by a substitute. When I saw replays of the challenge later, I realized that I had not fully appreciated its severity. I'd been too close. If I had been a little further away I hope I would have seen that it was a dangerous studs-up tackle, worthy of a red card. I put in a normal disciplinary report about the yellow but, in a covering letter, I told the FA that I thought I should have sent off Redknapp. He was charged accordingly and eventually suspended for three games – the same as if I had red-carded him during the game.

Incidentally, the following season, after years of discussion with FIFA, our FA changed the disciplinary procedure. FIFA wanted to stop so many red and yellow cards being reviewed later, so if a referee gave a yellow card during a game, it stayed a yellow no matter what video replays showed. So, a year later, Redknapp would have escaped suitable punishment.

But, getting back to Cahill, the Everton player had been incensed by the original decision only to caution Redknapp. Less than a month earlier (on 11 September 2004) Cahill had been sent off for receiving two yellow cards in Everton's match at Manchester City. His second caution had been for partially removing his shirt after scoring. So when I only yellow-carded Redknapp, Cahill commented, 'What's the game coming to? You can't celebrate but you can kick people.'

That issue – punishing fairly petty misdemeanours with the same severity as acts of violence or serious foul play – infuriates players, managers and supporters. But it is not the fault of referees, although they get much of the blame. Referees are like police, enforcing the law. They are not legislators, who make the law. They are not judges, who impose penalties according to the law.

The real issue should be the one illustrated so graphically by Schumacher's collision with Battiston: why do referees sometimes fail to enforce the law at all, and what can be done about it?

THE REF'S DECISION

Let's go back to the business about going for the ball, and even getting the ball, and it still being a foul. As the Law is now framed, many players, even top internationals, don't understand it. Many supporters don't understand either and if you stroll across any park on which matches are being played, you'll see fouls penalized by referees and hear mums and dads and other spectators yelling, 'He went for the ball!' If that is what you shout, then you used to be right, but you missed the Law change. You will also hear people yell, 'He got the ball!' That is often irrelevant.

If you tackle an opponent and make contact with him first before the ball, then it is a foul. It is not an alibi to say you didn't mean to touch the player. It is not an excuse to say that you honestly, genuinely went for the ball. If you make contact with the opponent first, then it is a foul.

So it stands to reason, I hope, that if you go for the ball but miss it entirely and catch the opponent it is also a foul. Sometimes it is a foul, even if you don't make any contact with the player – when, for instance, you jump in recklessly. It doesn't matter if you miss him. It doesn't even matter if you get the ball. It's a foul. In fact, if it's reckless it's a yellow card. If it involves excessive force and 'endangers the safety' of your opponent, it's a red card.

UEFA's guidance booklet for their international referees says this:

> **Any challenge involving excessive force, and therefore endangering the safety of an opponent, must be considered as serious foul play and the offender must be sent off.**

It doesn't mention the ball at all. It just talks about the nature of the challenge. It also does not give the referee any leeway. He must send off the offender.

The Law was not as clear-cut back in 1982, but in Schumacher's case he didn't have a leg to stand on – because he was jumping in the air towards his opponent. He wiped out Battiston. It was a foul and, to my mind, sufficiently dangerous for a straight red card. Corver can only have imagined that both men ran into each other, with Battiston being as much to blame for their collision as the goalkeeper, but Corver was probably the only person who thought that. What that shows is that referees will always make mistakes. That is self-evident. It is an oft-stated truism. But it is a central, unalterable fact of life and football.

However, I would like to see a system of 'citing' similar to that used in Rugby Union. When a player has got away with something on a rugby pitch, he can be 'cited' by someone afterwards and the incident is then reviewed. In football, the procedure would not be difficult. After all the weekend matches have been played, a panel of neutral people – probably some ex-players, a referee certainly and perhaps a former manager – would review incidents referred to them. Then serious fouls and acts of violence would not go unpunished and football would be fairer and better. An incident like the Schumacher challenge could be referred to the panel by the opposition, by the match referee after reviewing replays, or by the referee's assessor at the match. The panel would have suspended Schumacher; I am pretty sure of that.

I'd also like to see a sliding scale of punishments. At the moment, you get a one-game suspension for being sent off for two cautions and a three-game ban for being sent off for serious foul play or violent conduct. But I'd like to see many more options along a range of punishments, so that the worst examples of brutality are dealt with severely. I think that would ensure natural justice.

WORLD CUP STATS: 1982

QUALIFICATION TOURNAMENT: The number of places at stake in the finals was increased from 16 to 24. FIFA wanted more teams to qualify from North America, Africa and Asia. England's qualification campaign included defeat in Norway on 9 September 1981. On Norwegian radio, Bjørge Lillelien's excited commentary became world famous. He yelled, 'Lord Nelson, Lord Beaverbrook, Sir Winston Churchill, Sir Anthony Eden, Clement Attlee, Henry Cooper, Lady Diana, we have beaten them all, we have beaten them all. Maggie Thatcher, can you hear me? Maggie Thatcher! Your boys took a hell of a beating!' England still qualified.

FINALS: 13 June to 11 July. Twenty-four teams were divided into six groups of four. The top two teams in each group advanced to the second round, where they split into four groups of three. The winners of each group went through to the semi-finals.

HOSTS: Spain

MASCOT: Naranjito (an orange, wearing Spanish kit)

FINAL: Italy 3, West Germany 1

MATCHES PLAYED: 52

GOALS SCORED: 146

ATTENDANCE: 2,109,723

TOP SCORER: Paulo Rossi (Italy, 6 goals)

BEST PLAYER: Rossi

HOME NATIONS: England, managed by Ron Greenwood, were handicapped by injuries to key players: Kevin Keegan, Trevor Brooking and Bryan Robson. Yet they won all three group matches in round one. In their second-round group, they had goalless games against West Germany and Spain and so were eliminated without losing a match. Northern Ireland, managed by Billy Bingham, won their round-one group. Their 1–0 win against Spain (in which they had to play with ten men after the second half sending off of Mal Donaghy) is regarded as their greatest result of all time. In their second-round group, they drew 2–2 with Austria but were eliminated after losing 4–1 to France. Scotland, managed by Jock Stein, beat New Zealand 5–2, lost 4–1 to Brazil, drew 2–2 with the Soviet Union and failed to go beyond the first-round group stage. Their six goalscorers included two future Liverpool managers: Kenny Dalglish and Graeme Souness.

FIRST AID FIRST

ONE of the things that really surprised me watching the collision between Schumacher and Battiston all these years later is that Referee Corver appeared almost unconcerned about what had happened. The injured Frenchman was just left lying on his back.

Referees should react with urgency if someone is possibly seriously hurt. We are not trained as paramedics, but some refs do receive first aid tuition. When I was a young member of the very active and supportive North Herts Referees' Society, we received basic first aid training from members of the St John Ambulance.

Nowadays, the advice to referees is not to touch injured players. That is because of the fear that, if a ref inadvertently exacerbates an injury, he may be sued. But that mustn't stop a ref trying to help – speedy intervention might be life-saving. So I used to sprint up and make sure that the injured player was put in the recovery position and that his airways were clear. This is not the place to start giving readers first aid lessons, but basically the recovery position involves laying the patient on his or her side, with the arms and legs arranged in a specified way.

One of the good things done by our FA in recent years has been to introduce a charter for football clubs. Those who qualify for the charter have to have qualified first-

aiders at all their matches. The referee, however, should nonetheless act quickly when a player appears to be hurt.

STAMPING OUT VIOLENCE

One of the toughest calls a referee has to make is when a player treads on an opponent. Was it an accident? Was it something more sinister, and worthy of a yellow card? Or a red?

One of the methods top referees are taught to use in making that sort of judgement is to consider what might have happened if the two players involved were team-mates. So, for instance, when a player stands on an opponent, the referee should try to imagine what would have happened if they'd been on the same side. Could the player who trod on the other have avoided doing so if they were team-mates?

For instance, in the World Cup quarter-final in Gelsenkirchen on 1 July 2006, England met Portugal and Wayne Rooney met Ricardo Carvalho. Rooney trod on his opponent. Could the Englishman have avoided doing so? He said not, but referee Horacio Elizondo decided he could and sent him off.

In the following domestic season (on 14 October 2006 at the Madejski Stadium) there was a different interpretation when Reading's Stephen Hunt ran into Chelsea goalkeeper Petr Cech, who had dived to the floor ahead of him. Hunt's knee hit the goalkeeper on the head and led to a depressed skull fracture. Cech needed surgery. He had two metal plates inserted into his head and has played in a protective helmet ever since. Referee Mike Riley did not send off Hunt, so presumably he reasoned that the winger could not have avoided the collision, even if it had been a colleague in front of him.

I have to say I prefer Elizondo's more rigorous approach. I'd rather see a few players sent off in error than people get away with dangerous acts.

GETTING SHIRTY

Tim Cahill's complaint about being cautioned for removing his shirt as part of a goal celebration resonates with referees. The nonsense of having to give a yellow card for the way someone celebrates a goal was perfectly illustrated on 5 April 2009 at Old Trafford. Seventeen-year-old Federico Macheda came on as a substitute for Manchester United and scored a late winner in a thrilling encounter with Aston Villa. It was a stunning debut goal. He ran towards the crowd where his proud father was sitting and hugged him. For that, he had to be cautioned for celebrating with a spectator. Referee Mike Riley was not allowed to show common sense or any empathy with an understandably excited young man.

Less than two weeks later, on 18 April, Didier Drogba scored the winner for Chelsea in the FA Cup semi-final against Arsenal at Wembley, and whipped off his shirt as he celebrated. He knew he would be cautioned, and when referee Martin Atkinson (waiting at the halfway line so as not to make a provocative big deal) produced the yellow card Drogba accepted it with a smile and a shrug.

The mandatory caution for this offence is certainly no deterrent but it does place the referee in an invidious position.

BREAKING POINT

The injury to Battiston was horrific, but a referee should not judge the seriousness of an offence by the severity of the injury it causes.

For instance, on 4 January 2009, Southampton played Manchester United in the FA Cup at St Mary's and the home side had Matt Paterson sent off for a lunge at Nemanja Vidic. Paterson's studs thudded into Vidic's shin, yet the United player was not badly hurt. The ref was Mike Riley again, and I think he was correct to produce his red card that time. It was irrelevant that Vidic was not hurt. He might have been, because the challenge 'endangered the safety of an opponent'.

So it follows that when Arsenal's Eduardo Da Silva was fouled by Birmingham's Martin Taylor at St Andrews on 23 February 2008, the only matter for consideration by referee Mike Dean was the challenge itself, and not the outcome. Dean judged Taylor's challenge dangerous and sent him off. Eduardo suffered a broken leg and the damage was so severe that his bone was sticking out through his sock. Arsene Wenger, the Arsenal manager, said initially that he thought Taylor should be banned for life. Later, Wenger retracted that remark and accepted the principle of the point I am making: assessing the challenge should not be influenced by the seriousness of any injury – just as, on some occasions, the complete lack of any injury is irrelevant.

RED CARD FOR FIFA

WHEN I mistakenly only gave Jamie Redknapp a yellow card in 2004, I was able to report afterwards that it should have been a red. But FIFA changed the system soon afterwards. The game's world governing body decreed that, if a referee sees an incident and deals with it, then the case is closed. So if a ref gives a foul, but no card at all, there can be no subsequent additional penalty. If a ref gives a yellow card, it cannot be later upgraded to a red. The idea behind that change of procedure was that FIFA want the referee's decision to be final. They don't want games re-refereed later.

So, FIFA were very unhappy when our FA went against that decree to punish Ben Thatcher. On 23 August 2006 he was playing for Manchester City at Eastlands and appeared to use his arm on Portsmouth's Pedro Mendes. Just as I had missed a similar incident involving Thatcher when he was a Wimbledon player, so that night at Eastlands referee Dermot Gallagher did not realize what had happened. He booked Thatcher, but did not send him off.

Mendes suffered a seizure by the side of the pitch, where he had been dumped by Thatcher's challenge, and TV coverage of the incident led the FA to say that, because of the exceptional circumstances, they would charge Mendes with serious foul play (a sending off offence) despite the fact that he'd only been booked on the night.

I think the FA were right. Most people looking at the incident would have said to themselves, 'That has got to be more than a yellow.' Natural justice demanded that Thatcher should be punished properly.

Yet FIFA's attitude led to cautiousness at our FA and so an incident on 8 November 2008 resulted in what many believe was a miscarriage of justice. In a Football League Championship match at Oakwell, Sheffield United's Chris Morgan elbowed Barnsley's Iain Hume in the face. Hume was left with a fractured skull. Referee Andy D'Urso only showed Morgan a yellow card.

The severity of Hume's injury was not the issue, but the challenge certainly looked terrible on all the TV replays and most people who commented said he deserved a red and a suspension. The FA said, however, that there was insufficient evidence to proceed with a charge.

I'd like FIFA to understand that, while referees want their support, they want the leeway to upgrade yellow cards after matches have finished on occasions. As the Schumacher incident proves, referees make mistakes. We should let them rectify them when it is possible to do so.

RED CARD FOR FIFA (AGAIN)

BATTISTON received treatment on the field and then was carried off on a stretcher. That was entirely proper and understandable.

What many people don't understand – and certainly don't approve of – is why nowadays players who have been injured have to troop off to the sideline and stand there waiting to be waved back on by the ref.

Before that procedure was introduced, injured foot-ballers were just treated on the pitch and play stopped until they were fit enough to continue or able to go off the field. But players used to feign injuries. They did so for one of four reasons: to gain a free-kick, to persuade the referee to caution or send off someone, to take the pace out of a game and rob the opposition of momentum, or to waste time.

So FIFA issued an instruction (attached to Law Five, which deals with the duties of the referee). It says that all players who are injured must leave the field and play must restart without them. FIFA reasoned that players would be less likely to feign injury if they knew that they'd have to go off and leave their team at a numerical disadvantage.

What FIFA hadn't thought through was the underlying unfairness of this. I hurt you in a tackle, but you have to go off and I don't. That can't be right.

Then there are the special circumstances relating to goalkeepers. Law Three says that both teams have to have a goalkeeper. So, if you make one of them go off, a team-mate must replace him in goal, and must put on a goal-keeper's jersey to distinguish him from the outfield players. If the original goalkeeper comes back on, the guy who replaced him in goal has to swap shirts again. That can only happen during a stoppage. So the original goalkeeper might have to come back as an outfield player and wait for a stoppage to swap shirts and go back in goal. What a nonsense! So when they framed the law, FIFA stated that goalkeepers can stay on the field during and after treatment for injuries. Play stops until they are ready to resume.

A few years after introducing their instructions about injured players FIFA realized they needed to make another exception, in certain circumstances, for a team's recognized penalty taker. So, for instance, if Thierry Henry is brought down in the area and hurt in the incident, if would be unfair to make him go off and force his team to use a different player to take the penalty. So Henry could be treated on the pitch, get up, take the penalty (and very probably score).

But what about a free-kick taker? Shouldn't there be a similar special exception for him? And what about the big centre-forward who would want to be in the penalty area for the free-kick? Is it fair that he has to go off if he is crocked in the incident which leads to the free-kick?

It's all a mess. It's all wrong. FIFA should scrap their procedure – not least because referees get abused for making sure it is adhered to, even though refs (and this ex-ref) think it is daft.

R-E-S-P-E-C-T

Watching Schumacher clatter Battiston again (thank you, YouTube) I was surprised. It did not seem such a heinous incident as I remembered from all those years ago in the Gordon Craig theatre and leisure centre.

But as I watched it again and again, I realized that, yes, it was a shocking collision. I had been deceived, briefly, into thinking that it was not too bad because there was such a muted reaction by the French players. They milled about a bit, and one or two of them looked aghast at the referee, but by the standards of modern behaviour on the pitch, the French class of 1982 didn't seem overly upset.

Yet at the time, pretty nearly everyone watching was appalled by Schumacher's actions and their repercussions. So the probable truth is that the French players did react with anger and concern in the context of general behaviour at that time.

When I reviewed Geoff Hurst's goal in the 1966 World Cup Final, the lack of reaction by both sets of players was remarkable – to modern eyes. At the time, it was par for the course.

What has happened in the intervening years is that, imperceptibly, reactions and behaviour on the field have become ever more marked until they have reached the current level, where it takes very little to prompt an ostentatious, unrestrained show of outrage or petulant dissent. And when players believe they have been wronged, their behaviour is extraordinary. On 6 May 2009, for example, Chelsea's Didier Drogba went berserk after a series of contentious decisions by Norwegian referee Tom Henning Ovrebo in the Champions League semi-final.

We'll look in detail at that match, and the ref's performance, in the final chapter but on the general question of the tantrums by players, I acknowledge that referees are partly responsible. We didn't notice the gradual decline and didn't do enough to arrest it. The FA introduced their 'Respect Programme' in 2008 to try to turn the tide and turn back the clock, but it might be too late. Drogba's diatribe against Ovrebo was at the end of the season in which the programme began.

5

GOING BY THE BOOK

THE MATCH

To understand the expectation weighing down on Brazil at the 1978 World Cup we need to think how good their team was in 1970 and how disappointing they were four years later.

At the focal point of all their best moments in 1970 was the incomparable Pele, the person who called football *o jogo bonito* (the beautiful game). The 1970 team demonstrated what he meant. Every player was capable of great feats of skill and yet just as happy to play simple, effective passes. Brazil became World Champions for the third time playing this beautiful game and plenty of good judges believe the 1970 Brazilians set a benchmark for all time.

So imagine the global disillusionment four years later when Brazil played defensively, with plenty of fouling, and finished fourth in the World Cup. It felt like a betrayal of principles.

By the time the 1978 World Cup arrived, Brazil were again playing with zest and style, as the international television audience expected and hoped. They had a new genius, who was nicknamed 'The White Pele'. He was Artur Antunes Coimbra, known as Zico.

As Brazil took the field for the first time in the 1978 finals, two additional ingredients cranked up the drama. The first was that the tournament was in Argentina, a nation jealous of its neighbour Brazil's footballing renown. The second was that Holland's Johan Cruyff, the three times European footballer of the year, did not take part in the 1978 finals. That put the focus on Zico as the prime candidate to become the player of the tournament.

Brazil's first match was in the coastal city of Mar Del Plata. The José María Minella stadium had been built specially for the World Cup. The opponents were Sweden. There were fewer than 40,000 spectators in the relatively small ground but, around the world, armchair fans sat back. They had been beguiled in 1970 and betrayed in 1974. On 3 June 1978, they waited to be entertained by the boys from Brazil.

But the Swedes took the lead seven minutes before half-time. Thomas Sjöberg converted a chance created by Bo Larsson. The timing of Brazil's equalizer was interesting, considering what happened later. They made it 1–1 in the dying seconds of the first half through Reinaldo.

The score remained like that and then, in the last moments of normal time, Brazil won a corner, to be taken from their right wing. The referee, Welshman Clive Thomas, took up what, to modern eyes, looks an unusual position: inside the six-yard box, just behind the back post and no more than one step inside the pitch from the goal-line. Brazil changed their minds about who was going to take the kick and, eventually, the substitute Nelhinho got the job. But before he could take it, the linesman, Alojzy Jarguz from Poland, moved the ball. Nelhinho pointedly moved it again. Then there was a further delay as Reinaldo put himself in front of Ronnie Hellstrom, the goalkeeper. The Swede shoved him away with a hand in the small of his back and referee Thomas sprinted forward to have stern words with the keeper before going back to his position behind the back post.

Nelhinho took the kick. Zico sprinted in from level with the penalty spot. He connected with a clean header, the ball bulleted into the net and his momentum carried him in after it. Goal!

No. Not according to referee Thomas. At some stage in the proceedings – after the kick was taken but before Zico 'scored' – the ref had blown his whistle to end the match. As Zico picked himself up in the net, Thomas turned and pointed towards the middle of the pitch. He made a scissors movement with both hands – the international signal for 'No!' He pointed to his watch. He began to march off the field.

The 'goal' was not a goal. The match had ended at 1–1. The global audience, most of whom were willing Brazil to win, was stunned.

THE ISSUES

The decision by Thomas to blow his whistle when he did became notorious and raises a question that is fundamental to football and to refereeing: should the Laws be adhered to slavishly?

Brazil finished group runners-up behind Austria. So Brazil went into the much tougher second-round group and again finished runners-up. That meant they did not qualify for the Final, which was won by Argentina.

It is complete conjecture to speculate whether Brazil would have won the tournament if they had beaten Sweden. All we know for certain is that Brazil would have beaten the Swedes if Thomas had blown his whistle a fraction of a second later.

So let's get the Laws out. The relevant Laws are Five (The Referee) and Seven (The Duration of the Match). Part of Law Five says that the ref 'acts as timekeeper'. In fact, in 1978, it stipulated that the referee was the sole timekeeper. The 'sole' was taken out some years later, but the principle remains unaltered to this day. Law Seven says, in part, 'The allowance for time lost is at the discretion of the referee.'

When put together, Laws Five and Seven say that it is the ref who keeps a check of the time played and who decides how much should be added on for injuries and so on. Television coverage of Thomas's 1978 match showed that 45 minutes and 7 seconds had been played in the second half. If he decided that was the moment to end the match then, according to the Laws, he was perfectly within his rights to blow his whistle.

But what about 'Law Eighteen'? There are only seventeen Laws, but if you ask any ref about Law Eighteen, he or she will tell you that it is the unwritten Law – the one that says you should use common sense. Fred Reid, one of the two guys who examined me when I sat my refereeing test as a teenager, told me about Law Eighteen. I have told countless young refs about it since. Thomas seemed to have forgotten it.

His nickname in the British media was Thomas The Book. There were two reasons for that. One was that he did seem to have a predilection for taking the names of players – booking them. The second reason was that he always went by the book. He acknowledged both his nickname and the main reason for it by entitling his 1984 autobiography *By The Book*. In it, he describes the incident for which he is remembered around the world.

> **I looked at my watch and, with just seconds to go in my allotted injury-time, now coming up to thirty-one seconds, the corner was eventually taken. I blew the whistle after the ball had travelled about ten yards, turned and pointed to the tunnel to show that the match was over. Behind me there was uproar. There was a roar from the crowd, I saw the Brazilian players jumping for joy and I turned to see the ball in the back of the net, apparently headed in by Zico.**

Thomas's account reports extraordinary accurate – I would say impossibly accurate – time-keeping (although it does not tally with television recordings of the events). Thomas believed that, 'by the book', he was right to stop play precisely when he did. From the moment he ostentatiously pointed to his watch and strode away towards the tunnel until this day, he has maintained that it is not even an issue. The time was up. The game was over.

But in *By The Book* he says that, immediately after the match, Jose Maria Codesal, a Uruguayan official who was FIFA's referees' representative for that fixture, said it was a bad decision. Thomas adds, 'but he could not explain where I was wrong'. He also recounts that Jack Taylor, the Englishman who had refereed the 1974 World Cup Final, thought it was the wrong decision.

Thomas recounts that the Press were waiting for him at his hotel after the game. He says, 'I was quite prepared to take them all on but decided not to and, instead, went to bed. I slept the sleep of the just.'

The next day he was telephoned by Friedrich Seipelt, from Austria, who was a senior member of FIFA's referees' committee. Thomas reported the conversation in *By The Book*.

> **He said, 'You should have allowed the corner to be taken and awaited the outcome before terminating the game.' I told him that would have been dishonest as we would have been over time. I could scarcely believe him when he said bluntly that I would not have another game in the Argentine.**

Thomas never had another World Cup match anywhere. Yet he slept the sleep of the just and maintained that ending his game in any other way would have been dishonest. I think he was profoundly wrong.

His pedantry raises two related issues: credibility and the enforcing of the Laws of football. To have the former, a referee cannot always do the latter. Blowing the whistle on Thomas's whistle-blowing is the perfect way to explain what I mean.

Ask yourself how matches normally finish. Probably a goalkeeper has just fly-kicked the ball upfield, or has taken a goal-kick. The ball is in the air somewhere near the middle of the pitch and, lo and behold, the ref toots on the whistle and the game ends. Is it a coincidence that, after exactly 90 minutes and the precisely correct amount of added time, the ball just happens to be in mid-flight in the middle of the pitch? Do you suppose it is a coincidence that games end like that all over the country, week after week?

No. We all understand, without thinking, that referees end matches at convenient moments. They manage the situation and the game. It is a technique you learn very early on when you start refereeing. If you blow for time when one team is attacking, they complain that you have stopped them having a chance to score. If you whistle just as one team is about to take a corner, they will be shocked. If – Heavens forbid! – you whistle after the corner has been taken and the ball is in the air, they will think you are being deliberately provocative. So you learn. You allow attacks to finish. You permit corners to be taken and completed.

Some referees still get it wrong. Sometimes you will see a referee blow for time immediately after a bad tackle. The ref doesn't want to have to make a decision, or get his cards out. That is wrong. He should deal with the incident, restart play and then blow as soon as is practical and credible after that.

There are also occasions when common sense tells a referee not to add too many minutes. For instance, if one team is winning easily but things are starting to get a bit heated, the ref might think that the best thing for everyone is to end the match promptly.

You are trying to finish the game without any bad feeling, without controversy, with no surprises and when everyone feels it is right. You put practicality ahead of careful measurement of time. The same principle applies to ending the first half.

The next time you watch a game, try to guess when the referee will end each half. When the goalkeeper puts the ball down for a goal-kick, or is about to fly-kick it out of his hands, say to yourself 'When the ball is in the air, the ref will blow for time.' I bet you'll be right.

And here's the thing: there are countless other occasions during a match when a ref manages situations by not adhering rigidly to the Laws.

For instance, a good referee will change the tempo of his refereeing to suit the pace and ferocity of the match. If a game is getting overly physical, and there is a danger of tempers fraying, then the ref should crack down on every offence for a short while to calm everyone down. Once the ref has exerted his control, he might well be able to give fewer free-kicks so that the game can get going again. People will say, 'It's either a foul or it isn't.' But it is always a judgement call for the ref, and he should use that judgement to manage the match. The analogy I always use is of a simmering pot. If you get the heat just right the pot doesn't boil over and it doesn't go flat.

In *Seeing Red*, I talk about my 100th and final international fixture – the UEFA Cup semi-final second leg between two Spanish clubs, Sevilla and Osasuna, on 3 May 2007. Because of events in the first leg, there was a lot of tension at the start of my match, so I was determined to keep on top of every incident. I also changed my normal positioning and kept much closer to play. Whenever I blew my whistle and the players looked around, I was never more than a few metres away. The pot never boiled over that night.

Yet, if I was particularly strict then, it follows that there were countless times when I was far more relaxed – when I let a lot more go – so that the pot would continue simmering without going cold. It was all about practical, pragmatic refereeing. It was not about pedantically enforcing the letter of the Laws.

It also used to be the case that you needed to referee differently in Europe than in the Premier League. When I was first promoted to the FIFA list of international refs, and began getting games in places like Portugal and Greece, I went into matches with an English attitude towards tackling. If there was a slight bump between players, I'd wave 'play on', but then see that one of the players would be writhing about on the deck and that everyone expected me to stop for a foul. So I started giving fouls. That was what they were used to. That was what was credible in those countries.

Sadly, by the time I retired at the end of the 2006/07 domestic season, I had begun refereeing in the Premier League in a similar manner to the way I controlled games in Europe – because players in our League were going down without any real need and all the players expected me to give a foul.

When I refereed my first all-Spanish match (Real Sociedad v Atletico Madrid, UEFA Cup third round, 24 November 1998) both teams kept me hanging about in the tunnel while they deliberately delayed coming out of their changing rooms. They were trying to wind each other up, but they were messing me about as well. That influenced my attitude, I admit, and I went out and refereed it in an authoritarian manner – with 13 yellow cards and 2 reds. The assessor, an Italian called Tullio Lanese, said 'I do not understand. This was not World War Three. How can you show so many cards?' Gary Willard was my Fourth Official. He had a list of all the cautions and said, 'Well, which yellow card was wrong?' Lanese replied, 'None of them, and yet ...'

That remark by Lanese echoed what Codesal had said to Thomas. But, because Codesal could not tell Thomas where he was wrong in Law, the Welshman maintained that he must have been correct. When Lanese said what he did, I understood straightaway what he meant and accepted his point – which was that sometimes a ref has to have a feel for the game and respond to its nuances, and not just go by the book.

In 2006 Lanese was banned for 30 months after being accused of favouring Juventus in the Italian match-fixing scandal. But he had been right eight years earlier about all my cards in San Sebastian. I learned so much from what he said. I knew that I was wrong. No referee should leave the field after that many cards and think he has done well. Giving out 'more cards than Clintons' devalued their importance and showed that I was not managing the game. The cards lacked credibility. I had made the mistake of refereeing pedantically, to the letter of the Law instead of the spirit of the Game. A referee has to make decisions which are credible in the circumstances – and so he is governed by those circumstances and not just by the minutiae of the Laws. People will say, 'You must give everything you see.' But I showed in San Sebastian that if you do that, you don't have much of a game of football.

THE REF'S DECISION

So why did Thomas The Book apparently behave so officiously at the end of his match in the 1978 World Cup? The answer, I think, is in his character.

He was a successful businessman who ran an office-cleaning company. He was also a very, very competent referee who was selected for two World Cups and one European Championship. At the 1974 World Cup in Germany, he took charge of the first-round group match between Poland and Argentina on 15 June and the second-round group game between Brazil and East Germany on 26 June. Neither of those was a picnic, I can tell you, so he must have been well regarded. He was talented and had natural ability. He was not afraid to make decisions. But by 1978 I think he might have crossed the line between confidence and arrogance.

I am not alone in that view. Graham Kelly, a former chief executive of the Football Association, wrote in *The Independent* newspaper (on 12 February 2001) that the football authorities tired of Thomas when he 'began to adopt the role of a B-list celebrity'.

As a young ref, I was certainly aware of examples of what I thought was haughtiness by Thomas. One was during the League Cup Final at Wembley on 14 March 1981. Liverpool fullback Alan Kennedy fired in a shot and his team-mate, Sammy Lee, who was prone on the grass in the penalty area, ducked out of the way to let the ball pass over him and into the West Ham goal. Lee was in an offside position and the linesman flagged. Thomas dismissed the signal with an imperious wave and allowed the goal. We could debate whether Lee was interfering with play, but my objection was the way in which Thomas disdainfully discounted the linesman.

In *By The Book*, Thomas tells how proud he was that at the 1974 World Cup he gained a reputation as the strictest official. He also complains that, in 1978, referees did not have enough 'commitment' to take appropriate disciplinary action – except him. But perhaps the most revelatory disclosure in his autobiography is that he developed a habit of lifting a leg as he whistled for the start of a match. Thomas said he did his little kick as a gimmick, to make himself noticeable, to become, in his own words 'a celebrity'.

An autobiography is an opportunity to paint a self-portrait in words. I certainly regarded *Seeing Red* as a chance to try to explain how I saw myself. I sought to deal with what I believed to be misperceptions about me but I admitted plenty of mistakes. In Thomas's book – his self-portrait in words – he is unapologetic.

Perhaps Thomas's decision to end play as Zico was about to score was a horrendous error of judgement. Or perhaps it was to make a point. Perhaps he was exasperated with Brazil for fiddling about as they prepared to take the corner. Perhaps he was punishing them. It is even possible that Thomas blew his whistle when he did as a theatrical demonstration of his own importance.

I know there will be some for whom the words 'pot' and 'kettle' come to mind because I was frequently accused of being arrogant as a referee. But when I made my World Cup mistake in 2006, it shattered me. I could not sleep. When Thomas made his mistake he 'slept the sleep of the just'.

So the first conclusion about Thomas's match in 1978 is that referees must remember something. Kids or adults can go to any park and have a game of football of sorts. On the other hand a ref who goes to his local park and tries to have a game without players is in for a big disappointment. In other words, the adage that you can't have football without referees is not true. You can. But there is no point at all in having refs without football!

Referees must never think they are more important than the game. Some will say I sometimes lost sight of that. I don't believe I did. But what is certain is that the world sat down to watch Brazil in 1978, not Clive Thomas.

There is another conclusion to draw from the timing of his last World Cup whistle. It is that there must be a better way to determine the end of a game – because there is currently too much guesswork.

At the end of each half, Fourth Officials always hold up boards showing whole numbers. That is because referees always round up. If you think to yourself, 'It is three minutes and thirty seconds', you'd add on four minutes.

In fact, for me, the whole business of how much time should be added on at the end of each half was fairly arbitrary. It was the same for most refs. It still is.

When I first started refereeing, I had a stopwatch with three quadrants (45 minutes) highlighted. I put it in the pocket of my shorts and kept it running throughout each half. I also had a wristwatch with a stopwatch facility and I used to press 'stop' when appropriate. But, even back then, it was not a scientific process. I just stopped my watch when it felt right.

I often forgot to start it again. So I would furtively look at my other watch and try and work out how long the one on my wrist had been stopped. Later in my career when I had linesmen I'd ask one of them how long we had been playing. Most referees will tell you that forgetting to restart a watch is fairly common. So, in the end, you don't bother to stop your watch. You just glance at it when a stoppage starts (if you see what I mean) and look back at the watch when play resumes.

The Laws do not say that the ball must be in play for 90 minutes because it is recognized that there are natural stoppages – when the ball goes out for a throw-in, when a team is preparing to take a corner, even when there is a foul. The ref does not add on any time for those ordinary, short breaks in the action.

But Law Seven specifies some events for which time should be added (substitutions, assessment of injuries, players going off for treatment and time-wasting). The Law then adds the catch-all phrase that allowance should be made for 'any other cause'. In other words, the referee often has to decide what constitutes a stoppage and how long it is.

Additionally, in the Premier League, refs are told to add on time for goals (because the celebrations can be elaborate and time-consuming) and substitutions. The guidance is 30 seconds for a goal and 30 seconds for a substitution.

But the rest of the timekeeping is not very accurate at all.

For Thomas to assert that he knew how many seconds he was adding on, and that there were 31 remaining when the corner was taken, could be proof of how uniquely meticulous he was. Then again, perhaps he had made his calculations on the same arbitrary basis as the rest of us but decided not to give any commonsense leeway as the corner was taken.

I think football could learn from the two rugby codes. In Rugby League, there is a timekeeper in the stand who sounds a hooter when the required amount of time has elapsed. Play ends with the next tackle or when the ball next goes out of play. Similarly, in Rugby Union, although the referee signals when each half has run its course, play does not end until the ball goes out of play.

I'd like to see football have a timekeeper in the stand and a hooter to signal 'time up'. After the hooter, play would end when the ball next goes out for a throw-in, a goal-kick or a corner. You could not just end at the next stoppage in play – otherwise the team that was winning would just commit a foul to finish the match. The Law would have to stipulate that the game only ends when the ball goes out of play legitimately.

That would mean a fundamental change and different laws at the top of the game from those applied on parks pitches. There are not enough refs for grassroots games as it is, so you couldn't start introducing a neutral timekeeper as well. But football is already different at the top. In the parks there are no fourth officials, no technical areas, no stretchers and stretcher-bearers, but the game goes on.

The problem is, referees just estimate how long added time should go on for. So at the top of the football pyramid, let's call time on that guessing game.

WORLD CUP STATS: 1978

QUALIFICATION TOURNAMENT: Only 16 places were available in the finals. Don Revie, England's manager, quit during qualification to take a job in the United Arab Emirates. For the second World Cup in succession, England failed to reach the finals and Scotland provided the only British representation. There had been a military coup in Argentina two years earlier and there was much talk of some countries boycotting the finals. None did.

FINALS: 1 June to 25 June. Sixteen teams divided into four groups of four. The top two teams in each group advanced to the second round, where they split into two groups of four. The winners of the two second-round groups met in the Final.

HOSTS: Argentina

MASCOT: Gauchito (boy wearing an Argentina strip, a gaucho hat and a neckerchief and carrying a whip)

FINAL: Argentina 3, Netherlands 1

MATCHES PLAYED: 38

GOALS SCORED: 102

ATTENDANCE: 1,546,715

TOP SCORER: Mario Kempes (Argentina, 6 goals)

HOME NATIONS: Scotland had high hopes and an army of supporters. They took the lead against Peru through Joe Jordan. But they were stunned as Teofilio Cubillas scored three times. The result threw the squad into panic, which worsened when Willie Johnstone failed a drugs test and was sent home in disgrace. Then came a 1–1 draw with Iran. Scotland had to beat the Netherlands by three clear goals to qualify for the next stage. The game against the Dutch is remembered for a goal by Archie Gemmill, which many Scots regard as their greatest of all time. He won possession just outside the box, and jinked his way around three defenders before delicately chipping the ball over the goalkeeper. But Scotland only won 3–2 and were eliminated.

HANDS UP FOR JOE

Scotland reached the 1978 World Cup finals at the expense of Wales. They were both in the same qualifying group and the decisive match, on 12 October 1977, was at Anfield, because there had been serious crowd trouble at an earlier Welsh game in Cardiff. In the 78th minute, the ball reached the Welsh area from a long throw-in. An arm went up and a fist struck the ball. French referee Robert Wurtz awarded

a penalty. Television replays showed the offence had been committed by Joe Jordan's blue-shirted arm and not the red arm belonging
to Welsh defender David Jones. Don Masson scored, Scotland won
1–0 and went to Argentina.

Scottish fans revelled in the fact that England did not qualify and
Scotland manager Ally MacLeod bragged about his team's
prospects. So there was rejoicing in England when the Scottish
campaign became a debacle. One oft-repeated story is that, after
things started to go badly wrong, McLeod was pacing the grounds of
the team's hotel. A little dog ran up and the manager reached down
to pat it. 'This little fellow is my last friend in the world,' he said. The
dog bit him.

REPAIRING THE DAMAGE

When he blew the whistle to finish the Brazil–Sweden match so
contentiously, Clive Thomas ended his own World Cup career. He
also damaged the prospects of all British referees, because the
Brazilians were so upset by Thomas that they simply would not have
anything to do with British officials. No British referee was given any
significant appointment involving Brazilian teams from 1978 until
Dermot Gallagher took charge of the Under-20s World Cup Final in
1995 between Brazil and Argentina in Qatar. Gallagher did brilliantly,
and a lot of the damage done by Thomas 17 years earlier was
repaired at last.

RED CARD FOR ME

HAVING given Clive Thomas some stick, I must come clean about one of my many own mistakes. As a young referee I took charge of an FA Cup tie between Hereford United and Hitchin Town on 12 November 1994. It ended 2–2. The replay was on 22 November. I was born in Hitchin, and although I did not grow up there, the local paper made a bit of a fuss to welcome me back for the Cup game.

Hitchin won 4–2 but the match ended in farce because Hitchin scored their fourth goal right on the stroke of full-time. I just blew for the end of play, and nobody knew if I'd allowed the goal. I *had*, so Robin Fry, the chairman of Hereford, came into the dressing room and called me a cheat. That's what I contend he said, anyway.

I reported him to the FA. He told them he had actually called me cheap. They said that was still an insult and therefore an offence, but he said he wanted a hearing so we all had to go along to FA headquarters, which were at Lancaster Gate, in west London, in those days.

I didn't expect the hearing to last long, but Fry had a barrister and all the questioning went on for ages. I had to ask permission to go and feed the parking meter.

One of the assistants produced a written note of what had been said, and showed everyone the word 'cheat'. Fry was fined.

I don't know if that taught *him* a lesson, but *I* learned one.
I should have restarted play after the goal had been scored
and then blown up for full-time 20 seconds after the kick-
off. I should have been pragmatic and less pedantic.

YELLOW CARD FOR DUNNY

I CANNOT give my good friend Steve Dunn a red card, but he
must have a yellow for 'doing a Thomas' in an FA Cup tie. On
4 January 1998 at Selhurst Park, he blew his whistle for full-
time just as Marcus Gayle was heading a goal for Wimbledon against Wrexham. He had to disallow the goal and so the
match ended 0–0. The other Premier League referees all
joked with Dunny that he had done it so that he would get
extra money for officiating at the replay. His explanation?
Unlike Clive Thomas, Dunny accepted that he had made a
monumental mistake.

YELLOW CARD FOR ME

I DON'T think it was a red card offence, because the mistake
I want to tell you about was made with the best intentions
and did not lead to anything untoward – but it was still a
howler.

On 31 March 1999 I took charge of a friendly international between Holland and Argentina in Amsterdam. It was the biggest fixture of my career at that stage and a real test because it was the first time the two nations had met since a stormy game between them in the World Cup the previous summer.

Before the match I had to watch as Sepp Blatter, the FIFA president, presented the Dutch with their medals for finishing third at that World Cup. The Argentines had to watch as well, and did not look best pleased. Nor was I, because it was turning up the tension.

Yet at the end of the match, with the score 1–1, I allowed about five minutes of additional time. As I have said, it would not have been calculated accurately, but I thought it was about right.

Afterwards, Blatter had a few words of praise for me, but Mario van der Ende, a prominent Dutch referee who later served on FIFA's referees' committee, asked me what on earth I had been thinking about awarding so much added time. He felt that, at 1–1 in a friendly, I should have finished the match more promptly to ensure it would end without any trouble. The longer it went on, and the longer both sides sought a winner, the more opportunity there was for an incident to occur, he explained.

Months later, when I was on a referees' course in Europe, Volker Roth, the chairman of the UEFA referees' committee, made exactly the same point. He said that, particularly in friendlies, referees were mad if they added on more than two minutes.

I was wrong. I should have used practical, commonsense refereeing and not been such a stickler.

But it would have been better still if someone in the stand with a hooter had been in charge of timing.

 ## WHO'S THE DADDY?

JOSE Maria Codesal, the Uruguayan ref who told Thomas that blowing for time when he did so was wrong, had a son who refereed and whom I knew well: Edgardo Codesal Mendez. Edgardo married the daughter of Javier Arriaga Muñiz, the director of the FIFA international referee commission – so he was the son of one influential official, and the son-in-law of another. He refereed England's 1990 World Cup quarter-final against Cameroon and then the 1990 Final. Being that well connected cannot have hindered his appointment! By profession, Edgardo was a gynaecologist, which led to his receiving some inventive insults. But his dad was right about Thomas.

FINGERS FARCE

SYNCHRONIZING the timekeeping procedure between a referee, his assistants and the Fourth Official became straightforward after the introduction of microphones and earpieces. It used to be quite a palaver.

The theory was that the ref would ask one assistant to keep a watch running without stopping it at all, and would use him as a back-up. The ref would look over to him near the end of the half and the assistant would indicate how many minutes were left before 45 would be up. He'd do so by putting his hand on the side of his shorts and extending the appropriate number of fingers. When the assistant's watch had reached 45 minutes, he would signal to the referee by putting his hand across his chest.

Meanwhile, the ref would have asked the other assistant to stop his watch when there were stoppages in play. Towards the end of the half, the ref would look over to him too, and the assistant would signal how many minutes he thought should be added – again by displaying the relevant number of fingers against the black of his shorts.

In theory, the referee was only using the assistants to back up his own calculations, which he would then indicate to the Fourth Official. My instructions to the Fourth Official used to be, 'In the last minute or so of each half, put yourself where we can see each other and I'll either shout a number to you or indicate with my fingers how many minutes I'm adding on.'

It was a bit farcical, all that secretive use of fingers. If you watch carefully, you'll still see it used at those levels of the game where the officials are not wired for sound.

Steve Bennett had an even more elaborate system, involving his own tic-tac signs – a code in which putting his hand on one shoulder meant one minute, putting his hand on his head meant two. I am not sure where he put his hand after that! Now, thank Heavens, officials just talk to each other via their radios.

FERGIE TIME

Law Five does not say 'Sir Alex Ferguson shall act as timekeeper' but if Manchester United are winning, he starts jabbing his watch with his finger to let everyone know he thinks the game should be over. If United are losing, he is adamant that not enough time has been added.

On one of the first occasions I refereed at Old Trafford (on 21 August 1996) Duncan Ferguson scored twice for Everton in the first half. United hit back with a Jordi Cruyff goal after 70 minutes and a David Unsworth own goal 12 minutes after that. It finished 2–2. I had added four minutes in the first half and another five in the second – but Sir Alex thought there should have been much, much more and went ballistic.

The next time I was at Old Trafford, on 16 November 1996, Sir Alex had just celebrated ten years as United manager. I thought that, as a joke, I would take him a watch as a present. I didn't get around to buying one, but I told him what my plan had been. He said, 'Funny, because I was going to buy you a Mickey Mouse watch.'

He is by no means the only manager to try to pressurize the refs about the length of games.

Referees are not stupid. So when a manager makes a substitution during added time, and the player going off just happens to be on the far side of the field and probably hampered by a sudden stiffness in his legs, the refs know what is going on. The team concerned is trying to run down the clock, but the ref will just add on more time.

Some spectators and, shamefully, some commentators do not understand that when a Fourth Official holds up the board, the number displayed is the minimum amount of minutes the ref is adding. If there are stoppages or time-wasting during the added time, he should extend it.

That is why stadium clocks are all stopped at 90 minutes. They do not count down the added minutes because the ref often has to add some more.

YELLOW CARD FOR ME

THIS is my third card in this chapter (an appropriate number, I suppose) but I have to admit getting it horribly wrong at a Merseyside derby on 21 April 2000 at Goodison Park.

There had been no goals, and I thought it was time to end the game. So, as Liverpool goalkeeper Sander Westerveld shaped to kick the ball upfield, I turned towards the centre circle and blew my whistle. I expected the ball to fly over my head as I did so, but it never came. Westerveld's kick had struck Everton's Don Hutchison on the back. The ball ballooned up and backwards over the goalkeeper's head and into the net. I thought that my whistle had probably gone before the ball had entered the net but I didn't really know what had happened. I disallowed the goal. I had made a mess of the end of the game. I had literally taken my eyes off the ball.

SUDDEN ENDINGS

Abrupt, sudden endings to matches are not a good thing. There are many people who need to prepare for the end of a game – the gates have to be opened for people to leave, coach drivers have to move their vehicles, police and stewards need to be in position and so on.

If a referee needs to abandon a match because the conditions have become impossible then the police like to be warned in advance. Preferably, there should be a five-minute warning. The ref should tell the Fourth Official that he is going to abandon the game in five minutes' time and the Fourth Official can then alert the police. It happened when I was Fourth Official at Watford in my final season (on 29 December 2006). Steve Tanner was refereeing one of his first matches in the Premier League and I had been chosen as Fourth Official to give him some experienced back-up. Watford were drawing 1–1 with Wigan and torrential rain waterlogged the pitch. Using my lip microphone, I suggested that, although it was pretty obvious that the game would have to be abandoned, he should give me time to warn the police.

'NEXT GOAL'S THE WINNER!'

Because sudden endings are a bad idea, so was the 'golden goal'. That was the system introduced, briefly, to try to stop games going to penalties. If a match went to extra-time, then the first team to score during the extra period won the match there and then. It was like a school playground game when the bell has gone for the start of lessons and everyone agrees: 'Next goal's the winner!'

The system put incredible pressure on match officials because a big call in extra-time was effectively awarding the game to one side. For instance, on 28 June 2000, Portugal played France in the semi-final of the European Championships. In extra-time, assistant referee Igor Sramka (from Slovakia) signalled for handball by Portugal's Abel Xavier on the line. Referee Günter Benkö, from Austria, sent off Xavier and awarded a penalty. There was mayhem. Portuguese players pushed and shoved the match officials and their protests were so violent that UEFA later imposed suspensions totalling more than two years.

Eventually Zidane scored the penalty – the golden goal. France also won the Final with a golden goal, but the scenes at the end of the semi-final had been so disturbing that FIFA ditched the system.

WELSH BARRED

No Welshman is likely to referee in a World Cup as Clive Thomas did because officials from that country no longer take charge of top games in England.

The system used to be that referees in Wales and England were effectively amalgamated and a number of men from the Principality rose through the ranks to the top in England. They included Rodger Gifford, Keith Cooper, Howard King and Keith Burge.

But FIFA said that, as Wales wanted its own national team and its own vote on FIFA's law-making body, it also had to be regarded as separate as far as refereeing was concerned. So Welsh referees now have to ref in their own country and the highest level of domestic competition they can reach is the League of Wales.

Referees who were already on the English refereeing ladder were allowed to stay there – but not permitted to climb higher. The top Welsh referee at that time was Ceri Richards, who had reached the list of (English) Premier League assistant referees. He is still there. He cannot gain promotion and become a Premier League ref.

Richards did have one bit of luck, however. On the morning of the 2006 FA Cup Final (13 May), assistant referee Peter Kirkup woke up with an eye infection and could not run the line in the match – which was at the Millennium Stadium, Cardiff. The FA rang Richards at his home in Llanelli and asked him if he was doing anything. He said he was getting ready to go and play cricket. They invited him to be an assistant in the Final instead and, understandably, he put his cricket gear away and headed for Cardiff.

A GAME OF TWO HALVES

REFEREES should not end either half before 45 minutes have been played (or, in junior matches, the specified time for the age-group). If the ref realizes that he ended the first half early by mistake he cannot make amends by extending the second half. The 'additional time' at the end of each half is only to compensate for time lost during that half.

THE PENALTY CLAUSE

THE Laws of football specify one – and only one – circumstance in which the referee must extend the period of play. That is when a penalty is to be taken. Law Fourteen (The Penalty Kick) includes the sentence, 'Additional time is allowed for a penalty kick to be taken at the end of each half or at the end of periods of extra time.'

That's pretty straightforward, isn't it? Well, when does the taking of the penalty finish? If the goalkeeper saves the initial kick, but the ball rebounds to the penalty-taker, is his follow-up shot in time?

That is when commonsense, practical refereeing should be used again. For a start, you should not tell the players that you have added on time for the penalty. You should just award it and let them get on with taking it. Then you should let play reach a satisfactory conclusion. So, in the example of the penalty-taker scoring on the rebound, the goal should stand. Or, if the goalkeeper makes a save and his team hoof the ball upfield, it would be proper to end play then.

It is very different when a drawn game is decided by a penalty shoot-out. The Laws have a specific section for 'Kicks from the Penalty Mark'. It sets out where players can stand, and so on, and is entirely distinct from the procedure for 'normal' penalties during a match. During a penalty shoot-out, if the goalkeeper makes a save, the kicker cannot have a follow-up shot.

For 'ordinary' penalties, however, I would expect a referee to allow the whole of the penalty-taking 'move' to be completed before he blows for full-time. That is a perfect illustration of what I mean about ending a half or the game at the moment that feels right.

THE COVENANT OF THE ARC

THE Polish linesman, Alojzy Jarguz, delayed the taking of
the corner at the end of Clive Thomas's fateful match at the
1978 World Cup because the ball was not in the right place.
But the positioning of the ball for corners is another example of how some football fans don't understand the Laws.
An arc is marked at each corner of the pitch – a quarter of
a circle, with a radius of one metre. Fans yell when a player
from the opposition doesn't put the ball completely inside
the arc. In fact, it can be mostly outside the arc and still
be legal.

In football, any line is part of the area it defines. The
whole of the ball has to cross the touch-line to be out of
play, for instance. So unless the whole ball is outside the
arc, the corner can be taken legitimately. It is OK if the base
of the ball is outside the arc, as long as part of the sphere
of the ball is over part of the line. The next time you are at
a match and people yell at a player for not putting the ball
completely inside the arc, you'll know they are wrong – but
you might like to tell them under your breath.

BAD HOLDING ON CORNERS

When I speak at dinners or functions, one of the most common requests is to explain why referees allow so much holding, shoving and fouling at corners and other set-pieces.

I can explain it. But I can't excuse it. Penalty areas have become wrestling arenas – and that is the fault of referees, myself included. We allowed the situation gradually to progress to its current chaos.

It was bad enough in 2004 when José Mourinho, newly appointed as manager of Chelsea, invited me to talk to his players at the start of the season. I wanted to discuss holding at corners but the players thought it was part and parcel of the game and that there was nothing wrong with it. Since then it has only got worse.

It is a nightmare for refs. Strikers reach out behind them to be aware of where their marker is and grab a handful of shirt. Defenders keep 'touch tight', as they call it, to attackers. That *also* means getting hold of shirts. Meanwhile, half the players are not looking at the bloke taking the kick. They are looking at each other in the area, getting ready to block runs.

It is not an offence to look at someone. It is not an offence to stand between your opponent and where he wants to go. It only becomes 'impeding the progress of an opponent' if you move to block his run. And, although it is an offence to grab someone's shirt – we can all agree on that! – the ref cannot give a penalty or a free-kick unless the ball is in play.

That is one of the most difficult aspects for the referee: a lot of offences occur while everyone is waiting for the kick to be taken. The ball is not in play. So all a ref can do is delay the corner and give the offenders a lecture or perhaps caution one or two. The trouble is, it wouldn't be one or two. It would be five or six.

Now, imagine you are the referee. You've given the numbers nine and five a talking to, or a caution each, and so you are looking at them carefully when the corner is taken. Once the ball is in play, the nine and the five might let go of each other just as the kick is taken, and you'll miss someone blocking an opponent illicitly somewhere else. Or, you might whistle for a penalty for a foul by the number five, only to find, when you study the match DVD later, that he let go of his opponent just as the ball was kicked.

Let me give you a specific example. On 11 January 2009 at Old Trafford, Chelsea defender Ricardo Carvalho had hold of Manchester United's Cristiano Ronaldo from behind as the two of them ran towards the Chelsea goal at a corner. Carvalho let go of his Portuguese compatriot just as the corner was taken, but had already impeded Ronaldo's momentum enough to make him stumble. Ronaldo went down. Was it a penalty? No. The offence was before the ball was in play. But natural justice did not seem well served when referee Howard Webb gave nothing.

Jamie Carragher was working as a TV pundit and defended the defender. He said that Chelsea would have been unhappy with Carvalho if he had not been 'touch tight' to Ronaldo. When asked what would happen if referees started giving more penalties for holding at corners, he conceded that players would have to change their ways.

Interestingly, that point was borne out on 14 April 2009, when Chelsea played Carragher's own team, Liverpool, in the Champions

League quarter-final second leg at Stamford Bridge. Referee Luis Medina Cantalejo awarded a penalty when Branislav Ivanovic clearly held Xabi Alonso when the ball was knocked into the Chelsea area from a free-kick. From that moment on, there was no more holding at corners or free-kicks.

So it can be done, but it is extremely difficult for referees. And so, I am ashamed to say, they tend to give nothing and let the lawlessness continue.

Consider another case involving Webb. On 14 June 2008, he refereed Austria's European Championship match against Poland. Deep into added time at the end of the match he spotted a shirt-pull and awarded Austria a penalty. They scored to draw the match. In England most people, even our media, thought Webb had been entirely correct. But the Polish coach, Leo Beenhakker, said that Webb had wanted to demonstrate he was 'a big boy' and there was vitriol from the Polish media.

Webb did not get another match in those European Championships and he probably realizes that he should have sorted out all the penalty-area holding long before added time.

But then, all of us referees should have sorted it out years ago.

6

A TALE OF TWO PENALTIES

THE MATCH

There were three flag poles on the roof of the main stand of Munich's Olympiastadion on the day of the World Cup Final, 7 July 1974. On the centre pole was the Union Flag because an Englishman, Jack Taylor, was the referee. On the other two poles were the flags of the competing nations. West Germany, the hosts of the tournament, were playing against the Netherlands. The West German chancellor, Helmut Schmidt, was in the posh seats, near Prince Bernhard of the Netherlands. A billion people around the world were watching on television.

Taylor, the last Englishman to take charge of football's biggest fixture, had slept like a log the night before. But, in his changing room, in the slow hours before kick-off, tension began to build. He kept looking at his watch. He checked and re-checked things. Then, in the tunnel with the teams, he felt vulnerable and exposed.

Yet, in his splendid autobiography, *World Soccer Referee*, Taylor says that as he walked onto the field all his doubts left him as the nervous tension drained away. And then he delayed the kick-off because there were no corner-flags!

I think that is great. He was sufficiently calm, sufficiently focused, not to take anything for granted just because it was the planet's most prestigious fixture. Like a Sunday morning ref on a parks pitch, he had a good look around to make sure everything was in order. He spotted a member of the ground-staff sprinting away, obviously agitated, and realized something was amiss. Taylor immediately noticed that the corner flags were missing. He jogged from the centre-spot to the sideline to explain to someone what was going on (he didn't have a lip microphone or a Fourth Official, don't forget). Then he walked back into the middle, stood with his arms folded across his chest, shared a joke with the Dutch (who were waiting to kick off) and smiled broadly as a group of embarrassed ground-staff hurried out to the four corners of the pitch carrying flags.

Finally, all was ready for kick-off. Taylor, tall, upright, immaculately turned out and with hair as black as his kit, pressed a button on the watch on his left wrist and whistled for the Dutch to start. They played the ball back towards their own goal. Then it went sideways, across the line of four defenders. A total of nine slow, almost casual passes were played inside the Dutch half without a German even attempting to go near the ball. Then, as Arie Haan, a Dutch defender, looked up with the ball at his feet, Johan Cruyff – the best player in the world at the time – sprinted over. Haan gave way to the master and stepped back deferentially as Cruyff took possession, turned to his left and carried the ball into the German half.

Another sequence of passes began. Cruyff caressed the ball sideways and the ball was worked out to the Dutch left wing. It came back again to the centre-circle and was delivered once more to Cruyff. A total of 15 passes had been played since the kick-off. No German had touched the ball.

Cruyff jogged forward with the ball and then suddenly quickened his pace into a sprint. He sidestepped Berti Vogts, who span around and tried to keep pace with the Dutchman. Cruyff darted into the box, Uli Hoeness lunged feet-first on the edge of the area. Cruyff went down. Only 55 seconds had elapsed since the kick-off. And Taylor became the first referee to award a penalty in a World Cup Final.

The Englishman walked assertively to the penalty spot, turned his back on the goal and stood his ground waiting for the ball. As I have found reviewing other incidents, the lack of protest was quite extraordinary to modern eyes. Sepp Maier, the West German goal-keeper, stood disconsolately with his hands on his hips and the only player to approach the ref was Franz Beckenbauer, the West German captain. Beckenbauer made a couple of exasperated gestures and Taylor responded by waving him away. Four times the ref made the 'go away' signal. Later, reports of the exchange between the two men said that it concluded when Beckenbauer said, 'You are an Englishman.'

I know, from my own experience, that some Continental countries regard English referees as 'proper' to the point of pedantry. I am fairly sure that, by calling Taylor an Englishman, Beckenbauer meant that the penalty decision was harsh and officious. Perhaps he also intended the label as an insult, or an allegation of anti-German bias. At any rate, it was accurate; Taylor was English and proud to be so.

Beckenbauer retreated. Taylor placed the ball on the spot. Johan Neeskens took the penalty right-footed and drilled a shot straight into the middle of the goal as Maier, helpfully, dived away to his right. When the goalkeeper hauled himself up and picked the ball out of the net, that was the first time it had been touched by a German since kick-off.

Play resumed and there was plenty for Taylor to do. Then, with 20 minutes of the first half remaining, Wolfgang Overath carried the ball out of the German area, swayed away from a couple of opponents and swept the ball out to the left-touchline, where it was controlled by Bernd Hoelzenbein, lurking halfway into Dutch territory. Hoelzenbein switched the ball to his right foot and darted inside, accelerating towards the Dutch area. Wim Jansen slid in, feet-first. Hoelzenbein tumbled forwards. And Taylor became the first man to award two penalties in a World Cup Final.

Paul Breitner, his socks rolled down and with no shin-pads (which would not be allowed now) side-footed the spot-kick, like a pass, inside the left-hand upright. The score was 1–1. But the first-half drama was not over. As the seconds ticked down to the end of the half, the Germans piled forward once more and Rainer Bonhof cut the ball back from the right-hand byline. Gerd Müller overran the pass a little but trapped the ball, adjusted his body positioning and, on the half-turn, scored with a shot across the goalkeeper.

As the players left the field at half-time, Cruyff said something to Taylor. Then he said something else. And one more thing. So Taylor booked him.

There were strong appeals for another German penalty in the second half, but Taylor was unmoved that time and the score remained 2–1 to West Germany. Many of the Dutch were in tears at the finish as Beckenbauer lifted the new trophy to the sky.

THE ISSUES

Taylor certainly had an interesting afternoon and early evening in the Olympiastadion that day and there have been two subsequent allegations. Germans suggest he awarded the initial penalty because he wanted to make headlines. The Dutch claim that he awarded the second penalty to 'even things up'.

Those accusations are made about referees at all levels of the game but Taylor gave the first penalty for a very good reason: it was a penalty. And because he was 100 per cent right with that decision, there was no need at all for him to even things up later in the game. He gave the second penalty because he thought it was one.

Taylor was a brilliant referee. He refereed the 1974 Final without fear or favour. His decisions were motivated only by his determination to get them correct. But lesser referees and lesser men would have been influenced by the circumstances of that extraordinary day. And that issue – the human element of refereeing – is a big one for modern-day football.

So let's look at the first penalty. Let's start by putting the 1974 Final in context by stating the animosity some Dutch felt as fall-out from the Second World War. Willem Van Hanegem, who played in the match, was a baby when the war ended, but his father, two brothers and a sister died in the conflict. He gave interviews after the match in 1974 saying he hated Germans. This is not the forum for debating his attitude. But we should acknowledge it, because others shared it and that was a factor in attitudes towards the match, and to the refereeing decisions.

Pele had retired and vacated the spotlight, so it fell upon Cruyff, the slender, graceful and supremely gifted Dutch master. Brazil had temporarily forgotten how to play 'The Beautiful Game', so the Dutch were the team fans from other countries most admired. They were pioneers of a new concept: 'Total Football', in which any outfield player could play in any position and in which players switched fluidly between different roles during a game. It required a high level of skill and was glorious to watch. When Cruyff and his team reached the Final, neutrals wanted them to win it.

What did Taylor want? Like every referee I have ever known, he would have wanted a match in which he refereed well and got most of his decisions correct. He would have wanted 'a good game', because it is always more enjoyable to facilitate an exciting match. He would also have wanted to be seen to be fair and honest – and I am certain he was. There is no possibility of a referee reaching the very top of the tree if, at any stage, assessors and the people responsible for refereeing appointments suspect him of being swayed by bias or prejudice.

As for any notion that he wanted his place in history and so courted controversy, well that is something I feel strongly about, because that was the accusation thrown at me too many times. But Taylor had a very different attitude to me.

Let me explain by telling you about another referee who took charge of a World Cup Final: Pierluigi Collina, the bald Italian who, on 30 June 2002, refereed the Final between Brazil and Germany. I know him well. We've been at tournaments together and I am proud to call him a friend.

At the launch of his book, *The Rules of the Game*, I heard him asked, 'What is it like to referee a World Cup Final?' If I had been Collina, my answer would have gone on for about half an hour. I would have been able to remember details about the International Stadium in Yokohama, where the Final was staged. I would have been able to talk about standing in the tunnel, anticipating walking out. I would have said, 'I can still picture the pitch ahead of me, framed by the mouth of the tunnel. I can smell the grass. Over my shoulder, behind me, are the two most successful nations in World Cup history, Brazil and Germany.' And so I would have gone on, relishing the vivid memories.

Collina's answer was a lot shorter. He said:

> **To me the most important thing is to be consistent in the way I referee football matches. So I referee a game and, once I have done so, I leave it to one side and begin to concentrate on the next game. The World Cup Final is a match I have done, not a game I recall.**

The audience was left flat, but when you think about it, maybe that is why Collina was as good as he was. He just took each game as it came, to adopt a cliché beloved by managers.

Taylor had the same attitude. In 2006 he talked about 1974 and said, 'If you're in a game in the park with five people watching or at Manchester United you just accept it. Of course the World Cup Final was a vital game, but I focused on the match.'

I am sure neither Collina nor Taylor was really blasé about taking charge of World Cup Finals. I know Collina well, and I know what the

Final meant to him. I know that he was immensely proud of having been given the ultimate appointment, and so he should be. But both men obviously tried to treat the Final as just another game, and that worked for them.

I was a very different type of referee. I could never take it for granted that I was walking out at Goodison Park on Merseyside, or the Stadio Olympico in Rome, or any of the great theatres of football where I was fortunate enough to referee. The adrenaline rush motivated me and it was when those occasions stopped being special that I knew it was time to walk away from refereeing.

Some referees are always consistently eight-out-of-ten men. I'd average eight but I might get a ten for a big match, and then six for a routine fixture. I was known as a big-game referee. I relished the important fixtures. I rose to the occasions and wasn't afraid of making big decisions in them. So Sir Alex Ferguson said that when Manchester United had a crucial fixture, he wanted me to referee. I considered that a wonderful compliment.

I certainly took it as an accolade when I was appointed for United's match at Arsenal on 1 February 2005. The game between those teams earlier in the season at Old Trafford had seen Arsenal's long unbeaten sequence end in acrimony, and such was the rancour between the clubs that pundits predicted the return fixture would be unrefereeable. So the authorities gave it to me. It went really well, and I would rate it as one of my best performances as a referee. I had raised my game for the big Premier League showdown.

But I am forced to wonder whether, if I had been more like Jack Taylor and Pierluigi Collina, I would not have had such a calamitous conclusion to my own World Cup career. Perhaps a big game ref is not what you need for the biggest game of all. Perhaps if I were the sort to give a boring answer to the question 'What was it like to referee the World Cup Final?' I'd have had more chance of that question being asked of me for real.

But admitting that I wanted to referee 'big' matches is not the same as saying that I gave controversial decisions because I craved the limelight. The difference is something I deal with extensively in *Seeing Red*. Let me just say that it is possible to get close to the top of refereeing by being a Teflon Man; by having no controversies stick to you, because you don't make decisions. So, for example, if you think to yourself, 'Was that a penalty?', you don't do or say anything. The implication is that you couldn't see, and play continues.

But that is not right and I couldn't referee like that. It was more important to my self-esteem to try to get the big calls correct, and not be afraid to make them. That is not the same as wanting to be controversial.

Controversies are not created by the decisions, but by the media. If you give a questionable penalty against Lincoln City, very few people know. The 4,000 at the match will care, and the *Lincolnshire Echo* will chastise you, but that's it. So referees make decisions in Lincoln matches without having to think about a possible furore. But if you give a contentious decision against Manchester United, you know that Sir Alex Ferguson will create a storm, Andy Gray will pick the decision to pieces on Sky and Alan Hansen will shake his head and groan on BBC.

It is a fact of football life that referees are under massive pressure when they give penalties in the Premier League. That is what makes those decisions 'big' calls. But they still have to be made. So I don't agree with the adage that 'you don't notice good referees'. Taylor was noticed by everyone watching the 1974 World Cup Final – because he made some very big decisions and got them right.

THE REF'S DECISION

For me there is no doubt that the first penalty awarded by Taylor in the 1974 World Cup Final WAS a penalty. I am not so completely convinced about the second one. But we can ditch all the conspiracy theories.

For the first penalty, Hoeness was just outside the area when he lunged at Cruyff, but the contact was inside and with Cruyff, not the ball. Taylor was wonderfully well positioned, no more than three yards away and with an unobstructed view of the incident. So he gave the penalty; not because he wanted additional fame, not because he didn't like the Germans and not because Mars was in conjunction with Uranus. He awarded the penalty because it was a penalty. Taylor, the man who had been sufficiently unfazed by the occasion to notice that there were no corner flags, and who tried to treat all games the same, simply ignored the circumstances and got the decision right. As he recalled in 2006, 'The first penalty wasn't difficult to call. All I remember is thinking it was a 100 per cent correct decision.'

The second penalty was a tougher call, I would say. The most generous interpretation that can be put on Hoelzenbein's response to the challenge by Jansen is that he went down a tad more easily than was necessary. Another interpretation would be that he swallow-dived to the deck. That doesn't mean it was not a foul, but it did raise questions then and they linger still.

I've watched a German documentary about the Final, and in answer to the question about whether Hoelzenbein was fouled, the Germans say, 'Ja!' But I don't think that helps.

Taylor said, 'It was a trip or an attempted trip and the laws of the game are that's a penalty.' The Law he is referring to – Law Twelve (Fouls and Misconduct) – has changed since 1974. Then it included an element of intent. A player had to intend to trip someone for his action to constitute a foul. Now that element has been erased. If I trip you, even accidentally, it's a foul. But then, as now, it was also an offence to attempt to trip someone, and that is what Taylor believed was relevant.

Looking at the incident now, with the benefit of slow motion and different angles (none of which Taylor had, of course), it is quite clear that Jansen does not get the ball at all, but it is not as clear whether he gets the man. Taylor believes he did. In *World Soccer Referee* Taylor says,

> **As Jansen stuck out his leg to meet the threat, he just made contact with Hoelzenbein's boot. As Hoelzenbein went over I thought to myself, 'It's not as bad as you're trying to make it look, old son', but the Laws state that attempting to trip is just as serious an offence as actually tripping an opponent.**

Taylor then adds, 'Jansen was certainly not going for the ball.'

In 2006 Taylor said, 'What really does annoy me is the suggestion that I gave it to even things up.' As I say, Taylor believed 100 per cent that the first penalty was correct, and so had no reason at all to think, even subliminally, that anything needed to be evened up.

Nor is there any possibility that he was seeking headlines with either penalty decision. Giving penalties in a World Cup Final was not a big deal for Taylor, because he was striving to treat it just like any other match.

WORLD CUP STATS: 1974

QUALIFYING TOURNAMENT: Once more 16 places were available in the finals. Two were taken by the holders (Brazil) and hosts (West Germany). A total of 97 countries vied for the other 14. Goal difference (instead of goal average) was used for the first time when teams finished level in qualifying groups. Australia became the first country from Oceania to qualify for a World Cup finals. For the first time, England failed to qualify. They had been World Champions just eight years earlier, but found themselves needing to beat Poland at Wembley to progress from their qualifying group. Few expected England to fail and Derby manager Brian Clough, working as a TV pundit, described Poland's goalkeeper Jan Tomaszewski as a 'clown' before the game began. The 'clown' made a string of excellent saves, England drew 1–1 and were eliminated. The result cost

Alf Ramsey (later Sir Alf) his job as England manager. Britain was represented in the finals by England's gleeful neighbours Scotland.

FINALS: 13 June to 7 July. Sixteen teams divided into four groups of four. The top two teams in each group advanced to the second round, where they split into two groups of four. The winners of each group played each other in the final.

HOSTS: West Germany

MASCOTS: Tip and Tap (two cartoon boys wearing West German kit)

TROPHY: The Jules Rimet Trophy (which England had held aloft in 1966) had been won for the third time by Brazil in 1970 and awarded permanently to the Brazilians. So, in 1974, the current trophy was introduced.

FINAL: West Germany 2, Netherlands 1

MATCHES PLAYED: 38

GOALS SCORED: 97

ATTENDANCE: 1,774,022

TOP SCORER: Grzegorz Lato (Poland, 6 goals)

HOME NATIONS: Scotland beat Zaire 2–0, drew in a goalless game against Brazil, and finally drew 1–1 against Yugoslavia. While their match against the Yugoslavs was taking place, Brazil were beating Zaire 3–0. That was sufficient to eliminate the Scots. Their group was won by Yugoslavia. Brazil were runners-up. Scotland finished third on goal difference, were undefeated, but had to head home.

RED CARD FOR CARLOS

IN the opening match of the 1974 finals, between West Germany and Chile on 14 June in West Berlin, Carlos Caszely of Chile became the first player to be sent off during World Cup Finals with a red card. Red and yellow cards were formally introduced in the 1970 World Cup, but no players were sent off in that tournament.

The coloured cards were the idea of English referee Ken Aston, who was in charge of referees at the 1966 World Cup finals. Antonio Rattin's sending off against England in that tournament, when the Argentine refused to leave the pitch for several minutes, prompted Aston to think that there ought to be a clear, highly visible sign for sendings off. He hit on the idea of red and yellow cards while sitting in his car at traffic lights.

NEW BOY AT OLD TRAFFORD

The first time I refereed at Old Trafford, on 1 October 1994, was also the first time I had been there. I'd never been to watch a match or for any other reason. I was incredibly excited about it and travelled up to Manchester the night before the game with my wife, Julia. This was in the days when referees went to games in their own cars, instead of being taken there in a people-carrier with blacked-out windows for safety.

Julia and I stayed in a city centre hotel but the next morning I was awake ridiculously early and so on-edge that I was practically climbing the walls. For something to do, and because I always liked to have my petrol tank full when leaving a match, I decided to go and fill up.

Although it was several miles away from the hotel, I headed for Old Trafford and filled up near there. I just wanted to look at the place, and I was amazed to see the scarf-sellers and hot-dog vans setting up at eight o'clock in the morning. You can imagine how hyped up I was.

At Old Trafford, away fans sit in a corner of the ground, taking up part of the East and South Stands. Everton were the visitors that day, and were attacking towards their own supporters in the first half. Early in the game, as the ball was cleared out of the United area, I thought, 'Hang on, that looked like a penalty.' But by the time the thought had registered, play had moved on, and I didn't give it. I should have, but I wasn't experienced enough and was overwhelmed by the occasion.

But, over the years, I gained the necessary experience. I refereed more at Old Trafford than anywhere else, taking charge of 30 Manchester United home games and 3 FA Cup semi-finals.

There are basically two ways for refs to cope with huge occasions, according to sports psychologists. One is to shut it all out completely, to close your mind to the crowd and the stadium and to take football back to 11 players against another 11. The other is to embrace the reality, to acknowledge that there are 76,000 people watching in the stands, and to use that buzz to help you stay on your toes and do your utmost to referee well. Jack Taylor and Pierluigi Collina favoured the first method. I used the second.

I have to admit that I did not cope well with that first game at Old Trafford, but, with experience, referees can learn to deal with big occasions. In my last season, on 17 September 2006, I refereed at Old Trafford – and gave a penalty to Arsenal.

A SPOT OF BOTHER

On 21 March 2000 I refereed Portsmouth against West Brom at Fratton Park. I already knew that I had been selected for that summer's European Championships and that I was going to referee the FA Cup Final. Before the Portsmouth game, the assessor, Dave Frampton, said to me, 'I don't know why I am running the rule over you. You are flying at the moment. You don't need an assessor.' I replied, 'I'll tell you what I'll do. I'll make a deliberate error and see if you spot it.' I was joking. But there is a line between confidence and arrogance and that was one of the times I charged across that line.

Halfway through the first half, Steve Claridge, who was playing for Portsmouth, stumbled a bit after a challenge and I blew my whistle and pointed to the spot. He looked up and said, incredulously, 'It wasn't for the foul on me was it?' The home-end fans were silent. I had just given them a pen, but they knew it wasn't one and couldn't believe it. Mind you, Claridge's honesty didn't stop him taking the pen and scoring.

Gary Megson was West Brom's manager and he was apoplectic. The assistant referee on that side of the pitch, Jeff Pettitt, told me that I'd have to send Megson to the stand because he had gone way, way too far. So not only had I given a penalty that was wrong, I had sent their manager to the stand.

In the second half I sent off West Brom's Matthew Carbon, so nobody could accuse me of trying to even things up! I had made an honest mistake with the penalty and from that moment on I continued to make honest decisions – not favouring West Brom in any sense. I think that was the right thing to do.

A SPOT OF HISTORY

A meeting in London in 1863 formed the world's first Football Association and also agreed 'The Rules of Association Football'. The rules (not Laws at first, note) talked about 'free kicks' – kicks which could be taken without anyone impeding the kicker. There was no mention of penalties, but early newspaper reports of some matches referred to these free kicks as penalty kicks when they were given to penalize the opposition for an offence. In Rugby Football penalty kicks are still awarded anywhere on the field.

But in Association Football, the idea of what we now know as penalties – effectively a free-kick from a designated mark in front of goal – was invented by the FA of Northern Ireland and introduced into the Laws (as they had become) in time for the 1891–92 season. So, on 14 September 1891, the first ever penalty kick was awarded to Wolverhampton Wanderers against Accrington at Molineux. John Heath made history by scoring from the spot.

For several seasons, however, the Corinthian Football Club, one of the dominant English clubs of that era, refused to score from penalties on the grounds that to do so was ungentlemanly.

SPOT THE DIFFERENCE

What is the difference between a penalty taken during the game and one during a penalty shoot-out? Plenty. For a start, the Laws do not talk about shoot-outs. They refer to 'Kicks from the Penalty Mark' and they do so after the 17 Laws in a separate section headed 'Procedures to determine the winner of a match'.

Normal penalties during a game are dealt with in Law Fourteen, which specifies that only the goalkeeper and the player taking the kick can be inside the area as the kick is taken. Everyone else has to be outside the area, behind the 'penalty mark' and 'at least 9.15 metres (10 yards) from the penalty mark'. But the penalty mark is only six yards from the edge of the area – and that is the reason (and the only reason) why there is a line in the shape of a 'D'. It is an arc with a radius of 10 yards from the penalty mark and players have to stand outside the D.

For 'Kicks from the Penalty Mark' to decide drawn games, the goalkeeper and the kicker are allowed in the area, of course, and the other goalkeeper must stand on the goal-line but outside the penalty area. All the other players must be in the centre circle – which is why there is that long, nervous walk for each kicker.

Now, here is a question which I know is a good one, because I got it wrong once: when is a penalty finished? The question only applies to 'Kicks from the Penalty Mark' because with 'normal' penalties during a game, you just play on if the goalkeeper makes a save or the ball bounces back from the crossbar (the kicker can score on the rebound from the former but not from the latter). But what happens if the ball hits the bar or is saved during 'Kicks from the Penalty Mark'?

I used to believe that the procedure was completed once the ball had finished its forward motion. So, if it hit the bar and then bounced back into play, hit the goalkeeper and rebounded into the net, it was not a goal. I was wrong. The procedure ends when the natural phase of play ends. In other words, if you shoot and the ball hits the woodwork but then goes in off the goalkeeper, it's a goal. But if the goalkeeper parries the ball, the kicker cannot touch the rebound because if he did so it would be the start of a different phase of the action.

YOU'RE ALL RIGHT, JACK

I used to be convinced that Jack Taylor didn't like me. I was in awe of him, and so when our paths crossed, I probably tried too hard to impress him and was probably a pain in the backside – so I got the impression that he wanted to be somewhere else when he was in my company.

But after the 2006 World Cup we sat together on the top table at a dinner in Walsall and he said, 'I have been thinking long and hard whether it is the right thing to do to tell you this, but I have come to the conclusion that it is ... You know that as a former World Cup Final referee I have remained well connected with FIFA ... Well, you might have thought that you were in with a chance of being appointed for the Final in Germany but I know for a fact that you would have been. You had been pre-selected to do the Final.'

I was stunned and did not know how to react. I also wondered why he had decided to tell me.

He said, 'If you are the best referee in the world at some time in your career, you should know. You should not have to wonder. I want you to know. And I would have been delighted if you had refereed the Final, because it is about time another Englishman did.'

I have thought about that conversation many times. Would I have preferred not to know? No, he was right to tell me and I am pleased to have the information. It means that I know my mistake in 2006 really did do me some damage, but I also know that, for a while, I was up there at the top, and that is something of which I feel proud.

HOWARD'S WAY

Jack Taylor is a big, upright, impressive man and that must have helped his refereeing. Similarly, Pierluigi Collina is a striking-looking man and that gave him a strong physical presence on a football field which helped him exert his authority. He looked scary, I suppose, and that gave him an edge with the players.

My dad, Jim, was a big, powerful man, and so commanded respect as a referee. I have a smaller frame, but I hold people's eyes when I talk to them and I have a look which stops people dead. My kids will tell you about it. Before I became a professional ref, I am told people in the business world found me intimidating and I think I was able to use my physical presence on the football field to good effect.

Of the current Premier League refs, Steve Bennett is tall and commanding and Howard Webb definitely uses his physical attributes to give himself an aura of calm power. I noted that Howard began adopting very demonstrative gestures in the 2008/09 season. For instance, on 19 January 2009 at Anfield, he dismissed penalty appeals when Liverpool's Fernando Torres went down in the box against Everton by emphatically using both arms to make a gesture which clearly meant, 'No!'

Some refs would have done nothing, because you don't have to make any signal for not awarding a penalty. And not awarding a pen doesn't mean it is not a foul. It might mean that the referee could not see well enough to make a decision.

But on the occasion I am talking about, Webb made a big, dramatic gesture, waving both arms in front of him, parallel to the ground, like a huge pair of scissors. He was saying, 'NO, it's not a penalty. I didn't miss it. I saw it. It was not a foul.'

I thought that was an example of good, bold refereeing – and it was further proof that it is not true that the good referees are the ones you don't notice. Webb made sure he was noticed, because he had a message to deliver to the players and the crowd which he felt was important for his control of the game.

I have to declare an interest here, because Webb was supportive towards me when I was at my lowest ebb. On the morning after my mistake in the 2006 World Cup, when I knew that I had imploded in front of a global television audience, I sent text messages to every-one I thought I had let down. I sent one to Webb. He sent a very kind reply, along the lines of, 'You've got lots of big games left in you. Keep going.'

I would be overjoyed if Webb referees a World Cup Final. I had a chance, and was not able to grasp it. Nothing will change that, and so if Webb gets that far it won't make my hurt any worse. But it would be a very decent man getting the job and it would give refereeing in our country recognition and a lift. Webb should be focusing on the 2014 World Cup. That will be his best chance. As Jack Taylor said to me, 'It is about time another Englishman did it.'

THE BLACK COUNTRY BUTCHER

THE man who refereed the 1974 World Cup Final was John Keith Taylor. Jack was a nickname that stuck, but official records list him as John.

He grew up in a flat above the family butchers' shop in Wolverhampton, close to Molineux stadium, and eventually became a trained butcher himself and ran the business. That's quite a thought isn't it? He'd be chopping up meat in the morning, then he'd take off his white butcher's apron, head off to a match, change into a black kit and try to stop footballers chopping each other down. He needed a 'day job' because referees only got relatively small match fees at the time; certainly not enough to live on.

There is an anecdote about Taylor involving a match at Luton. He was hit by a flying penny from the crowd as he left the pitch after the game at Kenilworth Road. The comedian Eric Morecambe, who was a Luton director, went to see him to ask if he was all right. Taylor said he was fine and did not intend to report the incident. Eric said, 'Good. So can I have my penny back?'

At the 1974 World Cup finals, Taylor was in charge of the first-round group match between Uruguay and Bulgaria (a 1–1 draw on 19 June in Hanover) and the second-round group match between Argentina and Brazil (won 2–1 by Brazil on 30 June in Gelsenkirchen).

He was revered in world football before and after 1974. He officiated at the 1966 and 1970 World Cups and, on 2 June 1971, took charge of the European Cup Final at Wembley. That night Johan Cruyff was a winner. He was in the Ajax Amsterdam team that beat Panathinaikos of Greece 2–1.

At the end of his English refereeing career, Taylor closed his butchers' shop and spent two seasons refereeing in Brazil. Later, he coached referees in South Africa and Saudi Arabia and had a stint as commercial manager at Wolverhampton Wanderers before working for the Football League for many years.

On 1 February 1999, in Barcelona, Taylor was inducted into FIFA's 'Hall of Fame' and met two of the central figures of the 1974 World Cup Final – Cruyff and Franz Beckenbauer, who were part of the ceremony. Taylor produced a yellow card and brandished it at Cruyff, as he had done a quarter of a century earlier.

 ## FINAL COUNT

JACK Taylor is the last Englishman to have refereed a World Cup Final, but there have been others.

In the 1950 World Cup there was no Final, but England's George Reader took charge of the decisive game. The tournament was in Brazil, and the winners of four first-round groups went into a second-round group. A round robin of matches was played and the team at the top of the second-round group table (Uruguay) were the winners.

Reginald Leafe, Arthur Ellis and George Reader of England, plus Mervyn Griffiths from Wales, each took charge of a match in the second round – and Reader's fixture, between Uruguay and Brazil (on 16 July 1950) was the last and decisive game.

Leafe assessed me several times and Ellis became known to TV audiences as a referee in *It's a Knockout*.

In 1954, in Switzerland, the World Cup Final between Hungary and West Germany went to William Ling, from Stapleford in Cambridgeshire. Welshman Mervyn Griffiths was one of the linesmen and flagged for offside in the final minutes. Ling accepted his linesman's ruling and denied Hungary's Ferenc Puskás an equalizer that would have sent the game into extra-time. So Germany won 3–2 – and controversy continued about the decision for decades. There were no TV replays, but in 2004 a German TV channel discovered film footage that seemed to support the linesman, the ref – and the German victory!

CRUYFF'S CLEVER TURN

JOHAN Cruyff was born in Amsterdam and his mother
worked as a cleaner at the famous local football club, Ajax.
Young Johan joined Ajax's youth system on his 10th birthday but was not expected to have a big future because of
his frail physique. Yet he helped Ajax win the European Cup
in three successive years (1971, 1972 and 1973) and
became European Footballer of the Year three times (1971,
1973, 1974). Uniquely, I think, he has a football move
named after him: the 'Cruyff turn'.

 ## KAISER CHIEF

WE must not cast the Germans as the 'baddies' in our story
of the 1974 World Cup Final. Although the Dutch had tech-
nically superior individuals, the West German team also
included some excellent players. Gerd Müller, who had
been top scorer in the 1970 World Cup, was a predator in
the penalty area. Berti Vogts (who, years later, had an
inglorious spell as Scotland's manager) was a ferocious
competitor and there was Franz Anton Beckenbauer, nicknamed der Kaiser (the emperor) and probably the best
German player of all time. Beckenbauer, who played
mostly at sweeper, captained West Germany to victory in

the 1974 World Cup, was manager when West Germany
won it again in 1990 (beating England on penalties along
the way) and was chair of the organizing committee for the
2006 World Cup.

THANKS, DON

In his 1976 autobiography, *World Soccer Referee*, Jack Taylor quotes
the then England manager, Don Revie. He sums up what I say all
the time.

> Referees have the most difficult job in the world.
> They've got to make split second decisions and don't
> have the chance to sit back and ponder on what they
> should do. I fear that, at times, we managers feel
> referees should be absolutely perfect for 90 minutes;
> and that everything has got to be dead right every
> second of the game. Yet we can't get this as managers.
> We don't always pick the right team, carry out the right
> training method and book the right hotels. Players
> don't put every pass right, and coaches don't always
> bring youngsters through as they should. So, we're
> wrong in expecting referees to be perfect when we're
> not perfect ourselves.

FIXED PENALTIES?

I have something to say that I know will be provocative but that I know to be the truth. It is that referees let players get away with fouls in the penalty area. By that I mean that some challenges that you would penalize on the halfway line are not punished in the area. I am not saying that is right. I am saying that it happens.

If two players come together on the halfway line, and you think one of them has committed a foul, then giving the free-kick is a fairly inconsequential decision. You make the decision without hesitation. You give the foul.

But if the same incident is repeated in the penalty area, and it is an attacking player who might have been fouled, that is a much tougher decision because if you award a penalty you are usually effectively awarding a goal. Those decisions are less easy, and so are made less readily. You want a higher degree of certainty for a penalty than for a foul on the halfway line, so you set the bar higher. Minor fouls go unpunished.

In a sense, that is not being unfair, because the ref is consistent with both teams – punishing both for nearly all fouls well outside the penalty areas and not punishing either for minor fouls inside the areas.

It is probably true, as well, that if every slight foul in the area resulted in a spot-kick, it would kill the game, because there would be six to each side in every match.

But whatever justification I put forward, I know that it is not really right. It's just human nature, and refs are human.

RED CARD FOR RESEARCHERS

JACK TAYLOR'S first penalty, awarded to Holland, raised the question of bias. It is clear to me that he is not guilty of that charge, but it is an accusation that is levelled against all referees at some time or another.

In particular, there is a widespread belief in football that referees favour the 'big' teams, but there are two factors which are not taken into account by those who think that. The first is that decisions about penalties, offside goals and so on are more critical to 'little' teams. They are less able to fight back after conceding a penalty goal. They do not create many scoring chances, and so if a goal is ruled out, they suffer. So managers, players and supporters of 'little' clubs feel especially hard-done-by.

The second factor is that 'big' teams attack more and 'little' teams tend to defend fairly desperately – so the big teams win more penalties, and little teams collect more bookings and sendings off.

It is that second factor which is usually ignored by university researchers who, from time to time, seek to prove refereeing bias.

I am indebted to a gentleman called Peter Webb for comprehending the point I am making. He is involved in a company called Bet Angel and uses probability theory to advise on sports betting. He looked at the claim that Manchester United are awarded more penalties than their opponents – and found it to be true. But then he discovered the same was true of the Scottish champions (Rangers in the year he investigated). Then he found it was also true in every league he looked at. Instead of concluding that this showed a bias towards big clubs, he wrote, 'This seems to indicate that teams that are playing well and near the top of the league are going to be awarded more penalties on the basis of their attacking force and/or the opponents' defensive weakness.'

Yet still there is a widespread belief that research has proved refereeing bias. The most frequently cited research was conducted by a team from the universities of Bath, Otago (New Zealand), St Andrews and Bangor. They analysed all 2,660 matches in the English Premier League from 1996/97 to 2002/03 and published their findings in the *Journal of the Royal Statistical Society*.

The press release which announced the publication of their research, on 30 October 2006, made some very big assertions. It said, 'Football referees do favour home teams, study shows. Academics have proved what Premiership football managers have been complaining about for years – that referees are inconsistent and favour home teams.'

These researchers said they had devised formulae to take into account the fact that home teams attack more – although just how you can come up with an algebraic expression of what it is like to have Cristiano Ronaldo dribbling towards the Stretford End defeats me.

Just as importantly, I reject the researchers' methodology. They only looked at the number of yellow and red cards awarded. What about the number of fouls or the amount of penalties? What about the hundreds of decisions a referee makes during a game?

Having said all of that, I can think of circumstances when bias *is* demonstrated. It happens all the time in youth football, when a dad referees a game involving one of his children. If the dad is a decent person, then he will be determined not to show any favouritism – but, in guarding against it, he ends up being especially harsh on the team that includes his child or a little lenient towards the opposition.

A REAL CELEBRITY

In *World Soccer Referee*, Jack Taylor says,

> I can understand why some referees adopt a flamboyant, extrovert style for controlling a match. They like to think they are an important part of the game, and that the crowd likes to see them getting involved – everything I am opposed to.

Taylor was opposed to anything showy, and yet he was and is a real celebrity in the football world and a real gentleman.

7

BECKHAM'S HANGING OFFENCE

THE MATCH

Let's climb back into our time machine, set the dial for 1998, and watch as a fair-haired 23-year-old begins to make an international name for himself for the first time. That name, which will become known around the globe, is David Beckham.

He has such an amazing CV now – with a record number of England caps for an outfield player – yet, although he played in all England's qualifying games for the 1998 World Cup, the Manchester United starlet was out of favour when the finals began in France. Glenn Hoddle, the manager, accused him of not being properly focused and Beckham did not figure at all in England's opening fixture, a victory over Tunisia. He only came on as a substitute in the second match, a defeat by Romania.

England needed to win the third game, against Colombia on 26 June in Lens, and Beckham was recalled to the starting line-up. Hoddle's men took the lead after 20 minutes through Darren

Anderton, but the game was still finely balanced. Nine minutes later, following a foul on Paul Ince 25 yards from goal, Beckham took a free-kick. We all know about his prowess now, but then it was a stunning surprise as the ball whipped up and over the defensive wall and then swung and dipped into the goal.

England won and the victory put Hoddle's team into the knockout stages and set up a 'round of sixteen' showdown with Argentina – the first World Cup fixture between the two nations since that 1986 game when the South Americans had beaten England with the help of Diego Maradona and 'the hand of God'. Back home, all of England caught a bad dose of World Cup fever. The team had not qualified for the 1994 finals, but now they were one match away from the quarter-finals. Come on England! It seemed that every car had a sticker, a flag or some other way of showing support for the team.

English newspapers published diagrams to try to explain the physics of Beckham's free-kick against Colombia. Hoddle would have had a lot of explaining to do had he omitted Beckham for the Argentina match – but he didn't. On 30 June in Saint-Étienne, Beckham took his place on the right of midfield for the kick-off. At home in England, pubs with TV screens were overflowing with fans in replica shirts.

After five minutes those pubs resounded to groans. Goalkeeper David Seaman brought down Diego Simeone and Danish referee Kim Milton Nielsen signalled a penalty. Gabriel Batistuta took the kick, and scored.

Four minutes later, it was England's turn to be awarded a penalty. Michael Owen tumbled in the area as Roberto Ayala challenged, though contact seemed minimal. Had an Argentine forward gone down in the box with so little provocation we might have called it a dive. But it was Owen, and it was England, so we cheered as Alan Shearer thumped in the spot-kick.

Only six more minutes passed before Owen scored one of the greatest England goals of all time. He was in the centre circle when he received Beckham's pass. He immediately accelerated away from Jose Chamot and sprinted on and on towards the penalty area. Still hurtling along at exceptional speed, Owen swayed to his right and left Ayala flailing in his wake. Then, as goalkeeper Carlos Roa advanced, the 20-year-old England striker steered the ball past him into the net.

English euphoria lasted until just before half-time. Then Sol Campbell fouled Claudio Lopez, Juan Sebastian Veron tapped the free-kick sideways and Javier Zanetti scored. It was 2–2.

Just over a minute into the second half, Simeone clattered into Beckham from behind near the halfway line. Beckham was crouching slightly, preparing to receive the ball on his chest. The Argentine player jumped into Beckham's back, turning sideways at the last minute and struck the Englishman first with his left arm and then with the force of his entire body. Beckham was pole-axed and left lying face down. Simeone stumbled because of his forward momentum and the impact. Then, as the Argentine regained his balance and stepped backwards, Beckham, still on the floor, kicked him. The Englishman was face-down, with his knees bent and his two feet raised at right angles to the grass. He flexed his right knee so that the back of his right boot caught the back of Simeone's left leg. Simeone went down and stayed down, while his team-mates gathered to protest, and England players protested about the Argentinian protests.

The referee looked a picture of calmness. He strolled over, waved away players from both teams and repeatedly signalled for Simeone and Beckham to get up. He produced a yellow card for Simeone and then fished in his back pocket for another card. It was the red one. He held it aloft in front of Beckham.

Reduced to ten men, England were forced onto the back foot, although, with nine minutes remaining, Campbell did put the ball in the back of the net from an Anderton corner but the 'goal' was disallowed for a Shearer foul. That was the right decision, by the way. Sorry, but it was.

Extra-time came and went, and in the penalty shoot-out, Ince and David Batty failed to score from the spot. Yet nobody blamed either of them for England's defeat and elimination. Instead, the media rounded on Beckham, and so did most of the country. One newspaper headline the next day said, 'Ten heroic lions, one stupid boy'. An effigy of Beckham was hanged outside a London pub.

THE ISSUES

I watched the 1998 World Cup from England, but with a different sort of interest than I had felt about previous big football tournaments. I was an England fan, and was as excited as everyone else about seeing a good group of players represent my country. But by then I was a Premier League referee. I had made the international list in 1996 and the top group within that list in January 1998. I watched events unfold in France that summer thinking that I had a real chance of going to the next World Cup myself.

I had no real experience of how FIFA operated back then, but it was obvious to me, watching at home in England, that the 1998 World Cup referees had been instructed to enforce the Laws especially rigorously. That intrigued me, and prompted two related questions in my mind. Was it right to change the way the Laws were interpreted and administered for the finals of a major tournament? And was slavish adherence to the Laws the correct approach?

The Argentina game was one month and one day before my 35th birthday. My friend, near neighbour and fellow Premier League referee Graham Barber came round to watch the match with me at my home in Tring. He, my wife Julia and I settled down in front of the TV with a few beers. I'd like to apologize now, a bit belatedly, to the other families in our road for the noise we made with our cheering when Owen scored England's second goal and put Hoddle's team in the lead.

By half-time, Argentina were level, of course, and then our little group watched in fascinated horror as the television relayed the Beckham incident into the Poll lounge. As Simeone thumped into our player, either Barbs or I – I can't remember which – said, 'Yellow card!' Then, when Beckham flicked out his leg and kicked Simeone, Julia shouted, 'No! What has he done that for?' We two English refs exchanged exasperated remarks, saying things like, 'Stupid. He'll get booked as well now.'

When referee Nielsen flourished his red card in front of Beckham, Julia again shouted, 'No!' I am sure a similar reaction erupted in millions of English homes, and in the pubs it was probably less polite. But, as Barbs and I looked at each other as Beckham was sent off, our response was not one of shock or outrage. It was more exasperation. One of us asked, 'Did the ref have to?' The other replied, 'I suppose he was under instructions and had no choice.'

Like others in England, I was angry with Beckham. He had given the ref a decision to make. Nielsen maintains to this day that it was easy and correct – that he really didn't have a decision to make at all. We can all debate whether that's so, but the point is that the situation would not have arisen without Beckham flicking out his foot.

To Barbs, Julia and I watching in Tring, however, it did not seem that the situation was handled equitably. If Beckham was sent off, shouldn't Simeone have been shown a red card as well? Or, if a yellow card was sufficient for Simeone, couldn't Nielsen have shown Beckham a yellow as well?

If Simeone had not clattered into the back of Beckham, the England player would not have retaliated. Beckham's response, although unwise and not something football wants to encourage, was proportionate to what had happened to him. So, surely, the punishments meted out should have been proportionate. That would have been natural justice.

That brings us to a very difficult subject: even-handedness by referees. Even-handedness is different to 'evening things up'. I am not talking about doing something like giving a penalty to one side because you have already awarded one to the other team. I have talked about that in the chapter concerning Jack Taylor and the 1974 World Cup Final. I don't approve of that idea or condone it at all.

But I have to be honest and concede that refereeing can involve an element of doing things to be seen to be even-handed. Watch out for it at matches. If a ref sends a player off, he is likely subsequently to give a significant number of free-kicks to that player's team to show he is not biased against them. I must tell you that I managed my games by doing similar things to that. For example, if I booked several players from one side, I often found a reason to caution a player from the other side.

I didn't do that because of bias, and I didn't make up the player's offence, or book him for no reason. No, if a player from the team concerned committed an offence which might or might not be worth a caution, I just made sure it was a caution. That helped me manage the game and, ultimately, benefited both teams.

Some of you will consider that very wrong. Others will say, 'Ridiculous! Players either deserve a booking or they don't. Referees should not "find" a booking.' But, in order to keep control of a game, a referee needs to manage it, and sometimes managing a game means doing things – giving decisions or taking names – so as to demonstrate that he is not penalizing just one team. A ref 'finds' a caution or a free-kick so as to show even-handedness.

The worst thing you can accuse a referee of is bias, and so referees are anxious to show that they are free of it. I realize that proving a lack of bias by deliberately giving a decision to a certain team is a confusing, controversial concept, but I have to be honest and tell you that it does go on at the very highest levels of refereeing.

Refs are not instructed, 'If you've given three bookings to one team, find one for the opposition', but you learn as you go along that doing so helps manage the game and makes the yellow cards for the team who have got three more credible.

There was a good example of proving even-handedness on 8 February 2009 at White Hart Lane. Tottenham's Luka Modric fouled Arsenal's Emmanuel Eboue. It wasn't a particularly heinous foul, but as Modric went to move away, Eboue, who was still on the floor, lifted his leg and tripped the Croatian. The ball was in play some distance away, but referee Mike Dean, fearing that the exchanges between Modric and Eboue would get worse, stopped play and ran over to them. He had booked Eboue earlier and so, after showing him a second yellow card, pulled out the red. Then 'Deano' booked Modric. Arsenal fans probably thought, 'Eboue's only been sent off because he's already been cautioned. But he's booked both of them for this incident, so that's fair.'

I don't think that Dean would have cautioned Modric if Eboue had not retaliated. But once the Arsenal player responded to the foul, Deano felt (correctly, I think) that he needed to show both players yellow cards.

But it is crucial to emphasize that managing a game in that manner is not the same as evening things up after making a mistake. The difference is profound. Not once in my 1554 games did I ever think, 'I got that one wrong', and then later, up the other end, give something dubious to even things up.

My dad, Jim, was a referee and when I followed in his footsteps as a teenager one of the things he taught me was, 'If you have made one error, however bad it is, don't make another one to even things up.' So my philosophy became that, should I make a blunder, the only honest and correct thing to do was to strive even harder not to make another. My dad's tenet completely precluded the notion of giving a penalty, or something equally drastic, to 'even things up' – that would simply be adding a second mistake to the first.

One illustration of that attitude came at the Westfalenstadion in Dortmund on 25 February 2003. Real Madrid were away to Borussia Dortmund in the European Champions League and in the first half I waved away penalty appeals from Real. Ronaldo (not Cristiano, but the rather plumper, older footballer with that name) went down, but I didn't think it was a pen. Then at half-time I learned, from talking to Andy D'Urso, who was the Fourth Official and had seen a TV replay, that it should have been a penalty. So as we all came out for the second half, I told Ronaldo that I owed him an apology. He suggested that I owed him rather more: that I should give him a penalty. I said, remembering my dad's words, 'Up to now I have made one mistake. If I give you something you don't deserve it becomes two mistakes.'

As far as the Beckham sending off in 1998 is concerned, I believe that if I had been the referee I would have punished him and Simeone identically. In saying that, I am not ignoring the instructions given to Nielsen and the other refs by FIFA. But I am looking at the circumstances on the pitch and considering what I believe to be fair and equitable.

I don't think Beckham's kick was violent. But if it was, then Simeone's 'challenge' was just as bad. Simeone's actions might even have been premeditated. It happened soon after the start of the second half. Had Beckham's first-half performance been good enough to prompt half-time instructions to the Argentine players to 'get stuck in', to rattle him? A referee should be aware, at the start of the second half, that some offences will be pre-ordained in that way.

So if I was refereeing the 1998 match, and felt that FIFA's instructions gave me no choice but to send off Beckham, then I like to think I would have sent off Simeone as well. You could certainly make a case for red-carding Simeone for serious foul play.

As it was, Simeone stayed on the field and Beckham was dismissed. Argentina stayed in France. England came home. The flags were taken out of English windows and put away. The sense of deflation and abject dejection was palpable. As always, our nation dealt with disappointment by finding someone to blame. The Danish postal system was kept busy with mail from across the North Sea as many blamed the ref. But most Englishmen, women and children took their cue from the tabloids and blamed Beckham. The level of abuse he got was exceptionally harsh, even brutal.

His first match back in England was at the start of the following season: the Community Shield match at Wembley on 9 August 1998. Actually, it was called the Charity Shield in those days. I know, because I was the ref and I've still got the commemorative replica. Beckham's Manchester United played Arsenal, who had won the Premier League and FA Cup 'double' the previous season. I was appalled by the way Beckham was reviled by Arsenal fans; how the personal insults rolled down the stands and engulfed him on the pitch. I made a point of repeatedly getting alongside him and saying, 'Don't let it get to you David. Keep going. Keep playing. You're doing well.'

I was not showing him favouritism, merely empathy for a fellow human being and the spirit of football. I was also trying to ensure that he was not provoked by the abuse to do something stupid. I wanted to keep him calm so that the game didn't boil up and over.

Arsenal won 3–0, their final goal coming from 19-year-old Nicolas Anelka. But Beckham stayed on the pitch for the entire game, and although I booked three players, he was not one of them. They were Martin Keown of Arsenal and United's Denis Irwin and Gary Neville, since you ask.

Sir Alex Ferguson made sure that the Manchester United 'family' put their wagons in a circle and protected their young player from the critical media and abusive fans. With that support, Beckham began his rehabilitation and, as some of you might have worked out by now, that season following his World Cup sending off ended in extraordinary triumph for him and his club.

In the space of 11 days, United clinched the Premier League title by beating Tottenham 2–1 at Old Trafford (16 May 1999, referee G. Poll), then beat Newcastle 2–0 in the FA Cup Final at Wembley (22 May, refereed by my good friend Peter Jones) and finally, on 26 May in the Nou Camp stadium in Barcelona, scored twice in added time to beat Bayern Munich 2–1 in the Final of the European Champions League (refereed by the incomparable Pierluigi Collina).

Beckham played every minute of those momentous three matches at the climax of 1998/99, United's 'treble' season. In all he made 58 appearances for club and country that season. Yes, he collected eight yellow cards during the course of those games (none from me!) and yes he continued to receive terrible treatment from the fans of rival clubs, but that was largely because he posed such a threat to the teams they supported. By the end of the season the English public had begun to forgive and forget that rash moment in France.

THE REF'S DECISION

It is completely wrong that FIFA change the interpretation of the Laws for World Cup finals tournaments. Sometimes they amend the actual Law before the finals, and that is even worse.

FIFA's thinking is that the World Cup finals are their global show-case. So, if they want to crack down on something, like tackling from behind for instance, then they can make their point to the world by highlighting it at the World Cup. But when they do that they are saying to teams – and to referees – you all got here to the finals with one set of Laws and interpretations, but now we are going to change key elements of them. That is not right.

What's more, the Laws and their interpretation become a major issue, detracting from the football. The World Cup finals should be the best possible football spectacle, but FIFA spoil it by changing the ground rules and putting players and officials under new pressures.

Every year, new Laws are supposed to apply from 1 July. That is normally in the middle of World Cups and FIFA say it would be wrong to start using a new Law halfway through a tournament. Fair enough, but if FIFA are able to bend the system and introduce the Law early (at the start of the tournament, before 1 July), then they could bend it the other way and delay bringing it in until after the finals have finished.

Applying the Laws with extra rigour at World Cup finals is, in my view, equally wrong. By ordering referees to adhere slavishly to the letter of the Law, FIFA are in fact preventing good, practical, commonsense refereeing.

Every season in England, and probably all around the world, you hear people saying, 'Referees should be consistent.' But you also hear folk saying, 'Referees must show common sense.' Those two statements are often incompatible. In the search for consistency between different referees in different circumstances, the authorities sometimes set rigid guidelines and say that if 'x' happens, the ref must always do 'y'. But there will be occasions when a good, practical ref will ask, 'Why must I do y? Common sense, and the spirit of the game, tells me I shouldn't on this occasion.'

In December 1998, the BBC website carried a review of the year in which people who had been in the headlines during the previous 12 months were asked to look back at events. Referee Nielsen was one of the people interviewed and his comments shed revealing light on England's World Cup defeat. He said, 'England's game with Argentina was a big one and it was an honour for me to be part of it. Whatever had happened between the teams in the past was not important because a referee has to start from zero and focus on that game.'

He meant that whatever had happened before, he would start with an open mind. I agree that it is important not to prejudge individual players or their teams but I think it is a help, vital even, to know some of the issues and circumstances.

Nielsen went on, 'I have seen the game many times on video since, and I would not change any of the decisions. There were two early penalties, and the people who debate them forget they are only relying on a camera's angle. The referee is much closer to the action and can see things far more clearly than a particular camera angle. If there had been a camera on the opposite side to show the Michael

Owen penalty it would have looked a lot different. It is very difficult to use cameras and expect them to always show you the truth.'

Now that's an interesting philosophy: that a referee can see better than a camera. It is certainly true that slowed-down footage of events can distort them. It can make challenges look entirely different from what they were like in real time and real life. But it is also true that referees look at replays of incidents in the hope of exonerating their decisions – and when you watch something with that mindset, you often see what you want to see. In this case, what Nielsen seems to be suggesting about the Owen penalty is that although on TV it looked suspiciously like a dive, from another angle it was a nailed-on pen. As an England fan, I'm happy to accept that verdict!

On the red card, Nielsen said, 'The sending off of David Beckham was straightforward. The rules are very clear about kicking or attempting to kick an opponent. Many people today forget that it is a red card offence. Some have said it was only a soft kick, but that does not matter. In that situation one person has to be punished. If I had not sent him off, I would have been punished for not following the rules.'

Let's be clear about this: kicking or attempting to kick an opponent is, indeed, an offence that must be punished. It is one of ten offences for which a free-kick or penalty must be awarded. Despite what Nielsen said, it is not one of the seven red card offences.

So the absolutely key sentence is, 'If I had not sent him off, I would have been punished for not following the rules.' Nielsen believed that the instructions he had been given at the start of the 1998 World Cup finals meant that he had to send off Beckham. The instruction must have been to send off players who kick opponents, no matter how hard.

That upgrades the offence from a foul to a definite sending off, and is far too rigid, because Beckham's action was not 'violent conduct'. It did not warrant a sending off.

If Nielsen felt constrained by the instruction, he could have been even-handed. He could have taken into account the fact that Simeone's challenge might have been premeditated. He could have said, 'I have to send off Beckham, but I can make a case out for sending off Simeone as well.'

THE DANCING REF

Referee Kim Milton Nielsen was a contestant in the Danish version of the television programme *Strictly Come Dancing*. The public swiftly gave him his marching orders. He said, 'I was the first one to be voted off and it didn't come as a surprise. I was up against actors and singers who have nothing else to do, but I have a full-time job as an IT manager and my football career.'

His football career included sending off a second Manchester United player after dismissing Beckham in 1998. On 14 September 2005, in a Champions League match at Villarreal, United's Wayne Rooney clapped Nielsen sarcastically. The ref cautioned him for dissent and, because he had shown him a yellow card earlier, sent him off.

I know Kim reasonably well. He speaks English fluently, but it is not his first language and sometimes, when he tries to use irony, he doesn't quite get the inflections right. To those who don't know him that might make him sound aloof. In fact he is sociable and good company. He enjoys a drink and is a practical joker, but he is also astute and understands the politics of football.

To send Beckham off as he did, he must have known that he would be backed by FIFA; that the decision would earn him brownie points for being strong enough to send off an important player.

He started refereeing at 15, was on the FIFA list in his twenties and officiated at three European Championships, two World Cups and the 2004 Champions League Final between Monaco and José Mourinho's Porto.

The Champions League Final was one appointment I never achieved but, who knows, I might appear on *Strictly Come Dancing* one year.

LANGUAGE, GRAHAM

I was originally told I would be put on FIFA's international list in 1995, and if that had proved correct I might have made the 1998 World Cup. As it was, I didn't become a FIFA official until 1996 and the 1998 World Cup arrived too quickly for me. But in the build-up to the World Cup, I refereed Sweden's friendly against France (the eventual winners) on 22 April 1998. As Didier Deschamps kept his feet after a foul, I wanted to say, 'Play on', but in a confused attempt to communicate in his language ended up shouting, 'Vive La France!'

WORLD CUP STATS: 1998

QUALIFICATION TOURNAMENT: The tournament was expanded and 32 places were available in the finals. Four nations qualified for the World Cup for the first time: Croatia, Jamaica, Japan and South Africa. England had failed to reach the finals in 1994, but had reached the last four of Euro 96 (on home soil) and then won their World Cup qualifying group. Scotland qualified as best runners-up in the European qualifying groups.

FINALS: 10 June to 12 July. The thirty-two teams were divided into eight groups of four. The eight group winners and the eight group runners-up qualified for three rounds of knock-out matches which produced two finalists.

HOSTS: France

MASCOT: Footix (a cockerel in a France kit)

FINAL: France 3, Brazil 0

MATCHES PLAYED: 64

GOALS SCORED: 171

ATTENDANCE: 2,785,100

TOP SCORER: Davor Šuker (Croatia, 6 goals)

HOME NATIONS: Scotland lost to Brazil and Morocco. They drew with Norway but finished bottom of their group with one point. England beat Tunisia, lost to a 90th-minute goal to Romania and then beat Colombia. They were runners-up in their group but were eliminated in the next round, losing on penalties to Argentina.

A TEACHER AND A LESSON

David Elleray, a housemaster at Harrow School, was expected to be England's refereeing representative at the 1998 World Cup but, because he had been short-listed for promotion to the post of Headmaster, he decided he could not take the time off work. He didn't get the headship.

In his absence, Paul Durkin went to France for the World Cup. Before going he was in charge of the FA Cup Final (16 May 1998, Arsenal 2, Newcastle 0). A natural comedian and exceptionally popular among elite referees in England at the time, there was no prouder man in France than 'Durks' when the World Cup began.

He is also very much a family man, and it irked him that, in those days, FIFA did not provide any tickets for referees to buy so that family members could watch them in World Cup games. Before his first match in France – the group B match between Italy and Austria on 23 June – Durks was really upset that his father could not get a ticket to watch him, and was even more so when he stood on the pitch for the national anthems and saw row upon row of empty seats in the FIFA guests' section.

Whether that played on his mind or not, I can't say, but the match did not go well for him. Italy won 2–1, and Durks later confided in me that he didn't handle the situation well. He did not remain professional and calm. With that in mind, I resolved to stay calm and swallow all the criticism that came my way after things went wrong for me four years later at the next World Cup.

FACING A MYTH

A high-profile example of when a player's retaliation led to a sending off happened on 23 February 2008 when Liverpool played Middlesbrough at Anfield. There was a mild altercation between Liverpool's Javier Mascherano and Boro's Jérémie Aliadière, during which Mascherano grabbed his opponent's chin and Aliadière responded by slapping the Argentine.

Actually 'slap' overstates the contact. It was a sarcastic gesture, with only faint contact, but referee Lee Mason sent off Aliadière and took no action against Mascherano. Middlesbrough appealed against the sending off and Aliadière's automatic three-match ban. The FA not only upheld the suspension but also banned Aliadière for an additional game because they said the appeal was 'flippant'.

To me, both players should have been cautioned at most. Certainly, both should have been dealt with in exactly the same way, because Aliadière's behaviour was not worse than Mascherano's.

Somebody calling himself 'Grahamwrites' contributed a blog about the affair on the BBC website and said, 'The rules are clear, raise your hands to an opponent's face and you get sent off and banned for three games.'

You hear that assumption all the time – but it is another myth. There is no Law that says a player has to be sent off for 'raising his hands', even to an opponent's face. Law Twelve says it is a foul if someone strikes or attempts to strike an opponent. But it is only a foul. It is not even a mandatory caution, let alone a compulsory red card. And it is not necessarily a foul if it is just a slight, playful touch. It has to be a 'strike' or an attempt to strike. In practice, because we don't want everyone giving each other 'playful' slaps, if a player touches another player's face with his hand, a referee will nearly always give a foul and often a caution.

In the quest for consistency, some refs draw the line at the neck and say that any hand contact above the neck is a sending off, but that's not right.

The only relevant sending off offence is 'violent conduct'. For a punch, slap or 'raising his hands' to be worth a red card, there has to be violence. Of course, it is up to the referee to determine what constitutes violence, but it should be obvious to even the most ill-informed TV commentator that there is nothing at all in the Law which stipulates that someone must be sent off for 'raising his hands'.

RED CARD FOR PSYCHO

A MATCH in which sendings off caused me grief was on 31 January 2001 when Manchester United visited Sunderland's Stadium of Light. United were top of the League and Sunderland, managed by Peter Reid, were second.

United's Andy Cole scored but there were claims that he had handled. I hadn't seen anything wrong, so had to let the goal stand. I could not penalize an offence I had not seen. But the reaction of the players made me suspect it might well have been handball. Sunderland's Michael Gray gave me some abuse but I ignored him. When you think a team might have a genuine reason for being upset, you put up with a reasonable amount of dissent. You allow them a little latitude – far more than when you know you are spot on with your decision.

But Gray followed me all the way to the halfway line, swearing repeatedly until he said something so deeply offensive that I had to send him off. Later Cole and Alex Rae did that thing where players put their foreheads against each other, like rutting stags. Had they just touched foreheads, as players sometimes do, I would probably have booked them both. But I saw them both pull their heads back and then forward again in a butting action, and I had to send them both off.

The question a ref asks himself subliminally is, 'Are they just "adopting an aggressive attitude" or was there "violent conduct"?' The former is a yellow card. The latter is a red. That phrase 'adopting an aggressive attitude' is one we use in disciplinary reports, by the way. It is very useful.

My point here is that at the Stadium of Light I treated Cole and Rae the same. But that didn't persuade the fans that I'd had a good game. After the match I was told that 'people' were waiting for me outside. They had gathered around the match officials' people-carrier and I didn't imagine they wanted my autograph, so I was smuggled out and left the ground hidden in the assessor's car.

That was a bad day. So what constitutes a 'good' sending off? I'd say that if it is a good and, above all, correct spot, then a referee can feel he has done well.

One that I remember is pertinent to the Beckham sending-off in 1998 (because that was just after half-time and it is possible that Simeone had been instructed to 'get stuck in' to Beckham). The following season, on 31 October 1998, at St James's Park, Stuart Pearce, who was playing for Newcastle, was fouled just before half-time by West Ham's Trevor Sinclair. Pearce's nickname was Psycho, and not because he liked Hitchcock films. During the interval, in the ref's room, one of the assistants said, 'Psycho won't have liked that. He'll be out for revenge.'

Sure enough, three minutes into the second half, Pearce went up for a header and caught Sinclair in the face with his arm. I sent him off. On Sky TV, Andy Gray insisted it was an accident, that Pearce had been using his arms to help him jump and that it was impossible to jump without raising your arms. I even saw a Newcastle fan's blog in which he claimed I sent Pearce off to 'fix the game'.

I maintain that Pearce deliberately used his arm on Sinclair and that being watchful had enabled me to deal with him correctly.

 SEEING RED

I HAVE explained the controversial but important and justifiable refereeing tactic of 'finding' a yellow card for one side so as to be seen to be even-handed. There are also occasions when the ref 'finds' a red. That happens when you have used the yellow several times, but the game is still not under control. You say to yourself, 'OK chaps, if cautions won't do it, one of you is going to walk.' Again, you don't invent an offence, but if there is an incident which is on the cusp between a booking and a sending off, then the circumstances of the match push it over the line into a definite red card. English referee David Elleray was criticized for failing to adopt this policy in his only match at Euro 96. In charge of the game between Germany and the Czech Republic at Old Trafford on 9 June 1996, he booked ten players but did not send anyone off. Alex Ponnet, who was a referees' instructor for both UEFA and FIFA, told him he should have used a red. Had he done so, he might not have needed so many yellows. He would have taken control of the game, and it would have been a better spectacle. A yellow card is two things: it is always a disciplinary measure but it can also be a control valve. If you have used lots of yellows and still don't have control, 'find' a red.

FACT! ## TEAM TALK

BECAUSE Laws and interpretations of Laws are often changed for World Cups, FIFA used to ask participating referees to talk to competing teams. I had a meeting, for example, with Sven-Goran Eriksson, who was England's manager, ahead of the 2002 World Cup. Subsequently, however, FIFA felt the idea was unfair on those countries that didn't have a ref going to the World Cup, so they decided that every team should be briefed by a FIFA technical guy.

That doesn't mean that the English FA cannot invite Howard Webb (who will be our World Cup ref) to talk to the England players ahead of the 2010 finals and tell them what to be aware of in terms of Laws and interpretations. We should learn from what happened to Beckham in 1998, when he was the victim of a particularly robust interpretation of the Law. I would be very surprised if Fabio Capello doesn't invite Webb to talk to the players.

CARDS FOR CHRISTMAS

IN February 2009, referee Steve Bennett was caught by a newspaper sting. An undercover reporter recorded him saying that some footballers get booked deliberately in the build-up to Christmas to collect a suspension and have the holiday at home.

Every ref has heard stories like that, but no player ever came up to me and asked for a yellow card in those circumstances. Why would they need to? They could just grab someone's shirt and pull him to the ground in front of me. I'd have to get the card out, without necessarily knowing that I was helping his festive arrangements.

But on 12 March 2002, I was refereeing Real Madrid's Champions League match against Sparta Prague and Real defender Iván Helguera pushed an opponent over, looked at me and said, 'Card?' I didn't caution him but he did something very similar soon afterwards and the penny dropped.

At Champions League matches, referees are supplied with copies of the press information packs, and I always had a good look through mine. In particular, I noted the players who had asterisks alongside their names, which signified that they were one caution away from a suspension. Helguera had an asterisk and I realized that he wanted a caution and a suspension. Real had already qualified for the knock-out stage of the Champions League. He wanted to be suspended for a 'dead' group match so that his slate was wiped clean before the knock-out games.

I feared that he might do something reckless in pursuit of a yellow card and might hurt someone. I felt it was wise to give him a yellow as soon as I could. Real Madrid immediately substituted him. They didn't want him sent off. They just wanted him to collect the requisite number of cautions.

Perhaps the most famous example of someone getting booked on purpose involved David Beckham. On 9 October 2004, in England's World Cup qualifying match against Wales, he picked up an injury he knew was serious enough to prevent him playing against Azerbaijan four days later. He admitted, in an interview, 'I thought, "Let's get the yellow card out of the way."' Beckham committed a deliberate foul, was cautioned and so was suspended for a game for which he was injured.

SCALE OF JUSTICE

In Chapter Four, I said there should be a sliding scale of punishments for sendings off for serious foul play and violent conduct. It was Beckham's sending off in 1998 that helped convince me. As things stand, even a slight kick like that of Beckham on Simeone earns the same length of suspension as a two-footed jump tackle. That can't be justice.

Another, very similar, injustice occurred on 31 January 2009 at the Britannia Stadium. Stoke's Rory Delap hacked Manchester City's Shaun Wright-Phillips to the floor and then battered the ball against him. Wright-Phillips responded with a little, Beckhamesque retaliatory kick at Delap.

Referee Martin Atkinson saw the Delap hack, but not the Wright-Phillips flick. He sent off Delap and took no action against Wright-Phillips. Delap got an automatic three-game suspension. But Atkinson watched the DVD of the game and reported Wright-Phillips to the FA, who banned the Manchester City player for three matches – the same punishment as the Stoke man's.

Delap himself said that was unfair. 'It would probably be harsh for him to get banned from any games,' he observed. 'After what I did, his reaction towards me was to be expected really.'

BIN THERE

In March 2009, the International FA Board (FIFA's law-making committee) voted against experimenting with 'sin bins'. That was a disappointment. The idea of a 'sin bin' is that a player is sent off for a fixed period of time and then can return to the field. I'd like to see the system introduced for players who collect two yellow cards, when one is for a technical offence – such as not retreating 10 yards at a free-kick, or taking a shirt off to celebrate a goal.

Perhaps we could also send players to the 'sin bin' for abusing referees. That is currently supposed to be a red card offence, but refs seldom send players off for it. If the punishment was 'only' a temporary expulsion, refs would be more likely to invoke it and the problem might ease.

I would also decree that, once the sin bin expulsion period is completed, the referee should jog over to the player preparing to come back on and receive an apology. Players would hate that, but if they can't say 'sorry' then they should not be allowed back on. They'd soon start apologizing or, more likely, try really hard not to get put in the sin bin in the first place.

8

THE VEGETABLE PATCH

THE MATCH

From an English perspective, the biggest issue of the 1994 World Cup was that our team was not there. Four years earlier, the England team had lost on penalties in the semi-final, yet they were not even present in 1994, and the decisive qualifying match turned on a highly contentious refereeing decision.

On 13 October 1993, England needed to beat the Dutch in Rotterdam. Early in the second half, with the score still 0–0, England launched an attack. A long, lofted diagonal pass from the right touchline, just inside the English half, flew over the heads of the retreating Dutch defence and bounced in front of the galloping David Platt. He chested the ball forward and down and continued sprinting. As he entered the 'D' of the penalty area, an orange-shirted defender, Ronald Koeman, caught up with him, grabbed at his right arm and tugged on it. Platt tumbled forward into the area, but it was not a penalty – and that was not the issue. German referee Karl-

Josef Assenmacher produced only a yellow card instead of a red. That WAS the issue.

The true significance of the decision not to send off Koeman did not become apparent until the 65th minute. The Dutch had a free-kick on the edge of England's area, and Koeman drove it against the 'wall'. The referee ruled that Paul Ince had 'encroached' and so cautioned him and ordered the kick to be retaken.

On ITV television, commentator Brian Moore yelled, with mounting alarm, 'He's going to flick one! He's going to flick one!' But on the pitch, England were still expecting another pile-driver. Instead, as Moore expected but goalkeeper David Seaman did not, Koeman chipped the ball delicately into the net. A few minutes later, as England sought an equalizer, they were finished off by a Dennis Bergkamp goal.

The England manager, Graham Taylor, was furious that, instead of being dismissed, Koeman had remained on the pitch to score the breakthrough goal. Taylor well understood the significance of the result in terms of his employment prospects. The defeat by the Dutch meant that in the final round of matches England needed to beat tiny San Marino by seven clear goals and hope that the Dutch lost to Poland. In the event, England suffered further humiliation by conceding a goal in the opening moments before, eventually, beating San Marino 7–1. Holland beat Poland. Taylor resigned. England watched the 1994 World Cup at home.

THE ISSUES

Those who remember that era will know that Taylor was vilified by the English public, who took their cue from a vitriolic media campaign. I know something about being abused by football supporters and pilloried by the media, but in my lifetime nobody associated with sport has been subjected to such cruel denunciation as Taylor.

Memory played tricks on me as I attempted to recall the details. I assumed that the criticism of Taylor was mostly provoked by that defeat in Holland and England's failure to reach the World Cup finals, exacerbated by Taylor's increasingly distressed behaviour on the touch-line in Rotterdam – subsequently the subject of an infamous documentary. Further investigation, however, reminded me that, unbelievably, he was subjected to unprecedented and sustained media derision for 17 months before the crucial game with the Dutch.

Taylor took over as national manager immediately after the 1990 World Cup in Italy. Television coverage of England's progress to the semi-final of that tournament had led to a surge of interest in football. It made the game trendy. But that meant a lot more people were disappointed when England performed dismally in the European Championships in 1992. Needing to beat Sweden in the last group match to qualify for the knock-out stages, they lost 2–1.

In *The Sun* newspaper the next day a 'clever' headline appeared. It read, 'Swedes 2, Turnips 1'. The following day, picking up their own theme, the same newspaper published a photograph in which Taylor's head was morphed into a turnip. And from then on, whenever his England team faltered, he was pelted with various vegetable allusions as rival red-top tabloids sought to outdo each other in the savagery of their attacks.

The vegetables were put away after a defeat in Norway. Instead, under a headline reading 'NORSE MANURE', one paper pictured Taylor's head on a pile of steaming, fresh dung. That must have been an interesting assignment for the photographer. It was certainly an abhorrent attack on a man whose only crime was to fail to win enough football matches.

When the beleaguered manager took his increasingly forlorn squad to a summer tournament in the USA, results got horribly worse. On 9 June 1993, in Boston, Taylor's troops lost 2–0 to the USA, which was seen as a humiliation at home and led to another inventive headline; 'Yanks 2 Planks 0'. Taylor commented later, 'I was made to feel like Public Enemy Number One.'

I know that feeling, from my own experiences after the 2006 World Cup. But, tough though I found things, I was not under the media scrutiny that Taylor endured. I was ridiculed all right, but I was just a referee. He was the manager of the national team, carrying everyone's hopes, and as those hopes were dashed so the media maltreatment became increasingly vicious.

When Taylor's England resumed their World Cup qualifying matches, results did not improve and the pressure was really on him as the crucial fixture against the Dutch in Rotterdam arrived – and so now you can understand the significance to Taylor of referee Assenmacher's failure to send off Koeman.

He should have done so. Definitely. The Dutch defender should have been shown the red card. That is not open to debate, as far as I am concerned. But, it gives me an opportunity to clear up a few things.

Referees have an acronym for the type of offence Koeman committed. It is DOGSO, which stands for Denial of an Obvious Goal-Scoring Opportunity. It involves many myths and mysteries for football folk. I want to debunk the myths and solve the mysteries.

Let's start with that acronym: DOGSO. There has to be an obvious scoring opportunity which is thwarted by an offence. So, for instance, Harald Schumacher's foul on Patrick Battiston in 1982 was not a DOGSO because Battiston got his shot away before he was fouled. The goalkeeper's actions did not deny a goal-scoring chance. But Battiston could and should have been sent off for serious foul play – one of the other red card offences – and it might help us to understand DOGSO if we look at all the sending off crimes.

The relevant words appear in Law Twelve (Fouls and Misconduct). They say this:

A player, substitute or substituted player is sent off if he commits any of the following seven offences:

- serious foul play
- violent conduct
- spitting at an opponent or any other person
- denying the opposing team a goal or an obvious goal-scoring opportunity by deliberately handling the ball (this does not apply to a goalkeeper within his own penalty area)
- denying an obvious goal-scoring opportunity to an opponent moving towards the player's goal by an offence punishable by a free-kick or a penalty kick

- using offensive, insulting or abusive language and/or gestures
- receiving a second caution in the same match

Note that the introduction says 'is sent off'. The referee has no discretion. Note as well that in the two bullet points dealing with DOGSO there is no mention of that famous phrase 'the last man'. You will hear folk say, 'He shouldn't be sent off because he was not the last man'. Or they will say, 'He's got to go. He's the last man!' Yet the whole notion of 'last man' is one of the myths.

Often the player who commits a DOGSO is, indeed, the desperate last defender. So the idea has grown that if there is an additional, covering defender it cannot be a sending off. That is simply not necessarily the case.

For some reason as well, people attribute special significance to the presence of an outfield player as opposed to the goalkeeper. For instance, if a striker is clear through on goal and is hacked down from behind, most people will accept that it is a sending off despite the fact that there is a goalkeeper ahead of the attacker. Yet, if there is a defender on the line when a goalkeeper pulls down a player, people seem to think it cannot be a sending off.

Yet, if you think about it, a goalkeeper on his line has more chance of stopping a shot than a defender. And, if you consider the Law, neither the goalkeeper on the line nor a defender on the line is necessarily relevant. It doesn't matter who is on the line. It doesn't matter if there is a covering defender – or several! – the only consideration for the referee is whether an obvious goal-scoring chance has been prevented.

There is one other key phrase to which I want to draw your attention: 'an opponent moving towards the player's goal'. It is only a possible DOGSO if the attacker is going towards the goal. That is something many people don't know and something that causes ignorant criticism of referees.

All right, I'm talking about criticism I received. Specifically I am talking about two incidents in one match. On 8 September 2001, at the Riverside, I took charge of the North East derby between Middlesbrough and Newcastle. The home side were leading 1–0 in the first half when Middlesbrough goalkeeper Mark Schwarzer brought down Laurent Robert in the box. Robert had been going towards goal and it was a DOGSO. I sent off Schwarzer and gave a penalty. Middlesbrough took off an outfield player (Dean Windass) and sent on reserve goalkeeper Mark Crossley as a sub. His first task was to pick the ball out of the back of the net after Alan Shearer sent it there from the penalty spot.

Later in the first half, Newcastle goalkeeper Shay Given tripped Middlesbrough's Paul Ince in the area. The key element was that Ince was not moving towards the goal. He was on the six-yard line, facing the side-line, when he collected a loose ball. He took a stride in the direction he was facing (which, I repeat, was not towards goal) and was brought down. So I signalled for a penalty and showed a yellow card – not a red – to Given. Cue mayhem.

Home fans were incensed that Given had not been sent off because they thought he had done pretty much the same as Schwarzer. To make matters worse, from their point of view, Given then saved Jonathan Greening's penalty. I didn't get any Christmas cards from the Middlesbrough area that year.

The BBC website's report of that match, supplied to them by the Press Association, said this:

> **The turning point came towards the end of the first-half when referee Graham Poll sent-off Boro keeper Mark Schwarzer only to allow Newcastle's Shay Given to stay on the pitch for a similar offence minutes later.**

It was indeed a similar offence, but not an identical one. The direction in which Ince was running had made it significantly different. When it comes to DOGSO, the ref is just the dogsbody who enforces the Law. I had been right in Law, but very few people – players, managers, reporters or supporters – ever look at the Laws. I'm not particularly concerned that supporters don't do so. They know the basics and that is mostly OK. I am not advocating that you have to pass a test on the Laws to enter the ground. But surely the person who wrote that sentence on the BBC website should know the Laws. I would have thought that professional pride would have encouraged every journalist who makes a living writing about football to learn the Laws under which the game is played. But many not only don't know the Laws but they don't know that they don't know them, if you see what I mean. They blithely go on repeating the myths.

Of course, at Rotterdam in 1993, referee Assenmacher knew the Laws yet did not apply them. Then his error was compounded because Koeman scored the goal which put Holland on the road to victory. It was at that moment, when Koeman scored, that England manager Taylor became apoplectic in the technical area – and his terrible rage was captured in the Channel 4 documentary, *An Impossible Job*, which was screened some months later.

The documentary highlighted Taylor's manic behaviour during the game. For those of us who knew and liked Taylor, it was excruciating to watch, because he became almost incoherent with stress. When a pass went astray, Taylor said, 'Do I not like that.' It was a strange comment, spoken to himself but latched onto by the nation. It became a catch-phrase with which the media derided him.

There were several other moments in *An Impossible Job* that made very uncomfortable viewing. I remember thinking at the time that I wished Taylor had not agreed to cooperate with the documentary team. Yet, 13 years later, after my World Cup trauma in 2006, I agreed to make a television documentary with Garry Richardson of the BBC. I was driven by the urge to show people how difficult the 2006/07 season was for me and so, now, I have only sympathy for Taylor's decision to make his documentary. I imagine he was impelled by wanting the English public to appreciate the pressure under which the national football manager operates.

Every England manager is under that pressure, but none has been buried under such a sustained avalanche of abuse as Taylor. Steve McClaren became 'The Wally with the Brolly' after sheltering under an umbrella as England failed in their European Championship qualifying match against Croatia, but that was only one game. And McClaren almost fell into the England job, because he was assistant to Sven-Goran Eriksson when Eriksson stepped down. Taylor got the job because of truly remarkable achievements with Watford and then Aston Villa but, once he was England manager, Taylor had months and months of being reviled and defiled. No wonder he wanted a TV programme to help publicize that insane, almost intolerable pressure he was under.

THE REF'S DECISION

In 1993, when England lost in Rotterdam and Koeman was not sent off, I had just become a Premier League referee. I spoke at a lot of Referees' Association meetings around the country and members all wanted to talk about the Koeman incident. They all said, 'You'd have sent him off, wouldn't you Graham?' They asked the question rhetorically, because they thought the answer was self-evident.

But I always replied, 'I would like to think I would have sent him off.' I was being as honest as I possibly could. Although Koeman should have been red-carded, and although I hoped that I would have refereed the incident correctly, I could not be completely certain that I would have done so.

That was because there had been plenty of incidents in my career where I had made mistakes of omission – where, in retrospect, the decision seemed so clear-cut that it was a no-brainer, and yet I hadn't given it. I am not alone in that. The Fourth Official with whom Graham Taylor had several spats as England suffered their defeat in Rotterdam was Markus Merk. Eleven years later, the German was the referee when England played France in the European Championships in Portugal (17 June 2004). During that game, Wayne Rooney was bearing down on the French goal but was fouled by Mikaël Silvestre in the area. It was a clear goal-scoring opportunity – a DOGSO – but, like his compatriot more than a decade earlier, Merk did not produce the red card. Merk was a very, very good referee. He went on to ref the final of Euro 2004. So I would say that his failure to send off Silvestre illustrates that even the best make mistakes and so none of us can say for certain we would have sent off Koeman in Rotterdam.

I don't know what went through Merk's mind when Rooney was fouled, and I don't know what Assenmacher was thinking when he saw Koeman grab Platt's arm. Unless you are actually in the shoes of the refs at the key moments, you just cannot know what they saw, what they thought they saw, or what made them decide not to get out a red card.

In Assenmacher's case, he awarded a foul, so it was not a question of him thinking Koeman did not make a significant contact, or that Platt dived. It is just about possible that Assenmacher believed Platt did not have the ball under control, and so would not have scored. In those circumstances, Assenmacher would have convinced himself it was not a DOGSO.

The thing to remember is that once you have seen the incident a few times in slow motion, you have a very firm idea of what happened and then it seems obvious what the referee should have done. At the time, at normal speed and seen only once, it cannot have been so obvious to Assenmacher. That is all we can conclude.

If I cannot say for certain I would have sent off Koeman, then fans who have never refereed cannot say so either if they are honest. I repeat an important point for the Game: referees are human and even the very, very best will always make mistaken judgements occasionally.

There's another point I want to emphasize. I have said that the decision not to send off Koeman was the moment that defined

Taylor's time as England manager. By that I mean it was the turning point of the game, and Taylor is remembered for gibbering 'Do I not like that!' on the documentary. It was a cumbersome phrase that became the epitaph of his England reign.

At one point in the documentary, Taylor was shown shouting at the assistant referee, 'Hey! Hey! Tell your pal that he's just cost me my job.'

But I do not believe that the Koeman decision was what ruined Taylor's England career. Our qualifying campaign for the 1994 World Cup had gone wrong long before that. It started with a draw against Norway, it included a 2–2 draw against the Dutch at Wembley in which we squandered a two-goal lead, a draw against Poland in which we were outplayed, and that 'NORSE MANURE' defeat by Norway. At many points in the qualifying campaign, Taylor's England could have achieved results which would have rendered the 'Koeman game' unimportant.

Then, during the match in question, England did not lose solely because Koeman stayed on the pitch. They also lost because – among other things – they conceded a daft free-kick on the edge of the box and then didn't deal with it. David Seaman was caught flat-footed by Koeman's chipped shot, reaching out ineffectually for the ball as it sailed across in front of him. And then, soon afterwards, England conceded a second goal. So it is simply inaccurate to say that referee Assenmacher cost England a place in the finals, or cost Taylor his job.

Yet you hear the same faulty logic all the time. Managers, players and fans are always saying, 'That ref cost us promotion', or some similar, ridiculous claim. One decision might be important, but many elements combine over the course of a match – and many more over the duration of a season – to determine what happens to the clubs involved.

There is another point to consider. It is that unless a refereeing decision comes in the final minutes of the match, you cannot know what influence it has had. For example, let's think about the 'phantom goal' awarded to Reading at Watford on 18 September 2008. That was the occasion when the ball simply did not enter the goal, but assistant referee Nigel Bannister thought it had and referee Stuart Attwell believed him. Understandably, Watford fans were outraged. Because the game was drawn, they claimed the refereeing mistake had cost them two points. There are even some who will tell you that it cost Watford's Aidy Boothroyd his job, because he was sacked as manager just over three weeks later.

But the 'phantom goal' was the first of the game. The indignation of the Watford players and crowd acted as a spur, and the home team hit back with two goals to lead 2–1. They conceded a second, legitimate goal to Reading, who were riding high in the League, but how can anyone know what the result would have been without the 'phantom goal'?

By the law of averages and because he is human, referee Attwell must have made mistakes in Watford's favour. How can we know that none of them prevented a move that would otherwise have led to a Reading goal?

I certainly believe the adage that refereeing mistakes or controversies 'even themselves out during a season' but supporters forget those that go in their favour. For instance, England qualified for the 2002 World Cup finals courtesy of a last-gasp free-kick by David

Beckham against Greece at Old Trafford (on 6 October 2001). I think the decision to award the free-kick was wrong. It was never a free-kick – but you don't hear any England fans saying, 'Referee Dick Jol cost the Greeks victory.'

This is an important idea for referees, because they have to remember that one decision does NOT determine the outcome of a season. That is crucial, because otherwise the magnitude of the impact of decisions, particularly at the climax of a season, would weigh heavily on their minds. For example, my last game was the promotion play-off final in which Derby beat West Brom on 28 May 2007. Promotion to the Premier League was at stake, and rival newspapers came up with ever more madly inflated figures as they calculated how much the match was worth to the winners. It was called the £30 million match, then the £50 million match. I think it got up to £60 million. But I did not go out onto the Wembley pitch thinking, 'If I get something wrong it could cost one team £60 million.' I knew that both teams must have benefited from innumerable borderline refereeing decisions during the season and that those decisions had helped them qualify for the play-off final.

But football fans, managers and players are distraught after a defeat, particularly if winning would have confirmed promotion. It is human nature to want to blame someone. It is usually the ref.

There is one more point I want to make about which I feel strongly. The treatment meted out to Taylor by the media, particularly by the red-top tabloids, was shocking and unjustifiable.

Yes, Taylor was well paid. Yes, as England manager his job was to qualify for the World Cup finals and he certainly knew he would be criticized if England lost too many matches. So it was fair enough to criticize his management. However, it was completely out of order to make that criticism so cruel that Taylor's wife, daughters and parents must have been deeply upset.

I feel considerable empathy with him. I have seen my wife, Julia, hurt by things said and written about me. There were times when my mum rang me in tears about something she had read, or comments she had heard on phone-ins. I was always saddened beyond words when my loved ones were wounded by criticism of me. I have heard it said that Taylor was crushed by the knowledge that his parents were seeing him called a vegetable. I understand that pain, and firmly believe that the offending headlines and photographs which lay behind it are not the sort of thing a civilized country should find funny.

I have been told that Taylor's wife, Rita, was a great source of strength to him in his darkest days. That is something with which I can empathize as well, because my Julia helped me realize that family is more important than football.

There is another similarity between Taylor and me. We both now work in the media. Is that hypocritical on our part? I don't think it is because I make sure that I never forget when I write or broadcast that I am talking about real people, with families and loved ones. I am sure Taylor is the same, because he is an extremely decent man.

There is a natural inclination, I think, to try to redress the balance when you have been pilloried by the Press – to go into the media business and show that it is possible to make constructive criticisms when necessary without being abusive or personal.

I always remember, as well, that we are talking about football: a game. It is hugely important to me and I know that it is central to the lives of many, but it is a game. It cannot be right that Taylor was treated as badly, or perhaps worse, than a serious criminal. It cannot be right that referees are smuggled out of football grounds under a blanket (as happened to me twice). It cannot be right that I have been frightened for the safety of my wife, Julia, when she has left a ground with me. It cannot be right that Taylor's parents saw their son's head superimposed on a pile of horse dung.

You will have worked out by now that I like and admire Graham Taylor. I knew him when he was Watford manager the first time around. On one occasion he took a Watford team to play Tring Athletic to help them raise funds. I refereed one half and Graham Barber did the other.

I always got on with Taylor in those days and, since I have retired from refereeing, I have done some media work with him. We've been on radio together, and I've always found him to be one of the least pompous, most down-to-earth people you could want to meet. Perhaps that humility is part of the reason he was able to recover from the cruel treatment he received from the media when he was England manager. He was not sufficiently vain to be entirely wrecked when people criticized him. But that does not make the tone and intensity of the criticism right. It just demonstrates that Taylor's character was strong enough and admirable enough to withstand it.

WORLD CUP STATS: 1994

QUALIFICATION TOURNAMENT: Dramatic changes in the world were reflected by Russia competing for the first time as a separate nation after the break-up of the Soviet Union and Germany taking part as a united nation following the unification of East and West (the 1990 tournament had been won by West Germany, so strictly speaking this was the first time that the winners did not defend their title). The growing importance of Africa was highlighted by that continent having three places in the finals instead of one.

FINALS: 18 June to 17 July. The thirty-two teams were divided into eight groups of four. Eight group winners and the eight group runners-up qualified for three rounds of knock-out matches which produced two finalists.

HOSTS: USA

MASCOT: Striker (a smiling cartoon dog, standing on its hind legs, wearing football kit)

FINAL: Brazil 0, Italy 0 (Brazil won 3–2 on penalties)

MATCHES PLAYED: 52

GOALS SCORED: 141

ATTENDANCE: 3,587,538

TOP SCORERS: Hristo Stoichkov (Bulgaria) and Oleg Salenko (Russia), 6 each

HOME NATIONS: For the first time since they had begun to compete in 1950, no British teams reached the finals.

DINING WITH THE ENEMY

Each year The Football Writers' Association hold a tribute dinner at which they honour someone they feel has given special service to the game. In 2002, they honoured Graham Taylor.

I think that gala dinner demonstrates two things. The first is that Taylor rehabilitated his reputation after the terrible era of the turnip, the horse manure and the rest. The second is that he is a gracious man who was able to forgive those who had been so spiteful to him.

Taylor earned the England job because he was outstandingly successful with Lincoln, Watford and Aston Villa. After his England tenure he had a period in charge of Wolves and then his life turned a full circle when he returned to Watford and enjoyed another period of extraordinary success before moving on to Villa again.

Seven times during his career, he earned promotion. Twice he took Watford through the divisions to the top tier. Now he is an informed and informative broadcaster and writer and is back at Watford again, this time as non-executive director. The only period of his working life in which he was anything other than successful was when he was in charge of England.

Time is a great healer. I know that to be more than a cliché. I know it to be true. But I understand as well that when scars heal over they remain damaged tissue. I am sure that when something touches Taylor's scars – when something makes him think back to his days with England – there is still some pain.

But the way Taylor has dealt with the pain provides a stirring example to anyone who is facing or has suffered adversity. He did not run away. He resurrected his management career and then built a new profession as an articulate and thoughtful pundit. His example has been a real encouragement to me.

FACT! BALI HI

OTHER than Taylor (and almost every ref), the football people who have received the worst media treatment during my involvement with the game have been David Beckham after 1998 and Gareth Southgate after his penalty failure for England in the semi-final of Euro 96. For some reason, Stuart Pearce and Chris Waddle escaped quite lightly after missing penalties at the World Cup in 1990, and so did all the players who failed to score from the spot for us at the 2006 World Cup. There was no escape at all for Southgate. After his spot-kick was saved in 1996, he and his wife went on holiday to Bali. They visited an isolated Buddhist temple – where a monk went up to him and, in broken English, identified him as the man who had failed from the spot at Wembley.

 ## DO I NOT LIKE THIS

REFEREE Urs Meier would empathize with Taylor because he too was vilified by the English media.

In the Euro 2004 quarter-final between England and Portugal in Lisbon (24 June) he disallowed a Sol Campbell 'goal' because of a foul by John Terry on the Portuguese goalkeeper Ricardo Pereira. The score was 1–1 at the time, and if the goal had stood then it is highly likely that England would have won the match. Instead, they were eliminated on penalties after extra-time.

The English tabloids could not entertain the notion that we had lost because we were not good enough. They decided that we had been robbed by the ref. One headline called him, 'Urs hole'. Some published his email address – and he received more than 16,000 abusive emails. He also received death threats. One tabloid's reporters travelled to Switzerland and put a giant flag of St George on some grass near his home.

He was given police protection and advised not to go home. So, despite having been away for weeks, he could not see his family.

How can anyone justify that behaviour and that intrusion into his private life? How can anyone think it is an acceptable way to react to one decision in a football match?

And, by the way, the decision was correct.

FACT! BITE-SIZED INFORMATION

I HAVE my own reasons for recalling the stadium in which Graham Taylor did not like what happened to England. It was the Feyenoord Stadium in Rotterdam, which is known as *de Kuip* (the Tub). It was where I made my international debut as a match official. On 16 October 1991, I was an assistant referee and George Courtney was the ref for a European Championship qualifying match between Holland and Portugal.

I had never been to a match abroad, not even as a spectator, and it was an extraordinary adventure, unlike anything I had experienced. There was so much orange everywhere, for a start. It is the colour of the Dutch shirts and their fans wear orange wigs, orange hats, orange scarves, orange everything. I remember as well that there was a moat around the pitch and police with dogs. The dogs – fierce German Shepherds – were on the pitch side of the moat. That meant that they were literally inches away from me as I ran my line. I spent the entire match very aware that my ankles were bite-sized.

I remember as well that, on that trip, Courtney bought a Lladro figurine of a wizard, which I thought was appropriate, as in my view he was a wizard referee. I always called him The Wizard after that.

When I ran the line to The Wizard in 1991 I had ambitions, hopes and dreams, but I did not imagine that, nine years later to the day, I would be back at the Feyenoord Stadium as referee to the same two teams for a World Cup qualifying game. Yet that is what happened.

The stadium had been rebuilt substantially for the European Championships of 2000, but there was still plenty of orange about. I can't tell you, I'm afraid, whether there were any dogs patrolling the perimeter of the pitch, because as the man in the middle I didn't have to worry about whether there were or not!

 NOT SUPREME

DIANA Ross is one of the greatest recording artists of all time. She achieved world renown as a singer with an all-girl group called The Supremes and has sold more than 100 million records as a solo artist. But at the opening ceremony for the 1994 World Cup – held at Detroit's

Soldier Field stadium on the day before the tournament kicked off – she featured in a less than supreme moment. She was supposed to kick a ball into a specially prepared goal that had been rigged to collapse, the crossbar splitting in two and two posts falling outwards, as if her shot had been super-powerful. But she was wearing high-heels and, from a few yards, sent her shot wide of the post. It was a truly naff moment and, for many, confirmed their view that the Americans should not have been given the finals of a game they didn't understand.

 ## DISTANCE MEMORIES

TWO British referees were selected for the 1994 World Cup finals: Scotland's Les Mottram (who later became a professional ref in Japan) and Philip Don (who, when professional referees were introduced in England, was their first 'manager' – and so became my boss).

When I talked to Don about the 1994 World Cup he recalled that one of the biggest problems faced by all the referees was that the United States was so vast. They had huge distances to travel between matches as they criss-crossed the North American continent. Don's two games were nearly 6,500 miles apart – and he had other matches as Fourth Official.

The referees spent more time travelling than preparing for matches or recovering, and seldom went back to their central base. The USA was simply too big to stage a coherent tournament.

Similarly, from a refereeing perspective, it is a bad idea for two countries to co-host a World Cup if that means the match officials need two bases. That was what happened in Japan and Korea in 2002. We couldn't all get together to discuss matters and try to ensure consistency.

 ## CALLING FOR ASSISTANTS

THE 1994 World Cup finals were the first in which specialist assistant referees were used. There had been concern about the standard of decision-making by assistants in 1990 and an acknowledgement that the game had become quicker and that judging offside had become more difficult.

Only one English assistant went in 1994: Roy Pearson, from County Durham. He ran the line in five games, including the two refereed by his compatriot Philip Don. They were Saudi Arabia's 2–1 group stage victory over Morocco (25 June, Giants' Stadium, New York) and Sweden's victory on penalties over Romania in the quarter-finals (10 July, Stanford Stadium, San Francisco). In the semi-final, Don was Fourth Official and Pearson ran one of the lines (Italy beat Bulgaria 2–1 at the Giants' Stadium on 13 July).

Incidentally, Pearson was an example of someone who had more success as an assistant than as a referee. He showed an aptitude for running the line, but was perhaps not as confident in the middle. He once said, 'I didn't choose a career as a linesman, it just got created. Every time I had a flag in my hand, I seemed to do very well.' When he was initially appointed by FIFA, he was only refereeing Northern League matches, although he did eventually make it to the middle in the Football League.

THE REF WHO MADE FERGIE SWEAR

The 1994 World Cup Final was refereed by Sándor Puhl of Hungary. Because he comes from a country that is 'unfashionable' in football terms, and because it was his first World Cup, the fact that he was chosen for the Final demonstrates that he was a superb official. I certainly remember that he was awesome in the Final. He had to be, given that, in my view, neither of his assistants did very well and Puhl had to overrule them, correctly, on several occasions.

However, later in his career, Puhl gained a reputation for behaving imperiously, as if he believed himself to be infallible.

On 5 November 1997, he refereed Manchester United's 3–1 Champions League victory in Feyenoord (in the stadium in which England lost to the Dutch in 1993). Near the end of that game, Denis Irwin was badly hurt by a terrible tackle by Paul Bosvelt. Television coverage showed United manager Sir Alex Ferguson saying what looked like an extremely rude word. Yet Referee Puhl did not produce a card of any colour, and so after the game UEFA officials urged him to look at a video of the incident. They wanted him to admit that he had missed a red-card foul so that they could then charge Bosvelt and get him banned. Puhl refused to look at the incident again.

In *Seeing Red* I say that I believe I handled my 2006 World Cup humiliation better than I might have handled success. If I had refereed the Final, I think I might have let it go to my head. I think Puhl showed that it can happen.

9

FLAGGING IN JAPAN

THE MATCH

I learned the names of the referees for the 2002 World Cup finals by looking on the FIFA website. The European contingent was listed first, in alphabetical order, with 'Pierluigi Collina (ITA)' at the top. Number 11 of 13 was 'Graham Poll (ENG)'.

So this is not the story about something I watched in a bar in Stevenage or in the lounge of my home in Tring. I was there for this controversy. No, not the one involving Croatian defender Josep Simunic and three yellow cards. This is another one involving him four years earlier.

Referees work hard at getting their positioning right, so that they can see offences clearly, but sometimes a match official can be too close to a serious incident to appreciate everything that went on. There are moments in life like that: you are involved in some incident or other and you can only see it for what it is at the time. It is later that you get a better perspective, comprehend its significance and realize how it is perceived by others. That is what happened to me in 2002. I had a leading role in the controversy of the 2002 World Cup, but I did not realize it when my scene in the drama was played out. My part in the plot-line – and many people still think there was a plot – came in the game I refereed. There were two highly contentious moments, but it was afterwards, as events unfolded in other games, that a conspiracy theory took root.

Having tried to put myself in the boots of the refs at the centre of the other controversies we have revisited, I invite you to put yourself in *my* place this time. To do that you need to imagine how proud I was to see myself on that list of officials for the planet's biggest football event – only then will you be able to comprehend how desperately disappointing it was when things went so wrong in my first game, to the point that it proved to be my only one of the tournament.

The 2002 finals were the first in Asia and the first hosted jointly by two separate countries, Japan and South Korea. I was among the refs based in Japan and in *Seeing Red* I tell the story of how, initially, I was supposed to take charge of Japan against Russia. But, because I had some history with the Russians, they objected and, after some hasty and embarrassed rescheduling by FIFA, I was switched to the Group G fixture between Italy and Croatia in the one-year-old Kashima Stadium on a Saturday evening (8 June).

Kashima is in an area called Ibaraki, on the coast and within commuting distance from Tokyo. I had been to the ground three days earlier to watch Kim Milton Nielsen ref Germany's 1–1 draw with the Republic of Ireland. Another reason for my being there then was to run the rule over Jens Larsen, one of the assistant referees, who had also been assigned to my match. My other assistant was to be Phil Sharp of England, whom I knew very well, of course. I remembered that Larsen, a Dane, had run the line at the Euro 2000 final but he had produced a poor performance as linesman in the Germany–Ireland match. That meant he would need an outstanding assessment in his next game to restore his reputation, which worried me, because often that means an assistant will go looking for a big decision. That is not what a referee wants.

My concerns were not helped at all by the amount of stick Larsen got from the FIFA match observer at the formal debrief in front of all the other refs and assistants back at our base. I reasoned that Larsen would probably feel he really needed to make some big calls to prove himself in the next game. My fears grew worse when the same observer, Carlos Alarcon of Paraguay, was appointed for my game. Then my anxiety was ramped up even more when Alarcon's last words to Larsen before kick-off were, 'Be strong.'

I didn't want him to feel he had to be strong! I wanted him to be calm and confident, yes. But I did not want him seeking to impress anyone about his 'strength' by making a dramatic intervention.

It was a demanding game but it went reasonably well at the start, and the score stayed 0–0 until five minutes into the second half. Then came the first incident that was to haunt me.

I was well up with play, seven or eight yards outside the Croatian area and about a third of the pitch inside the left-hand touchline. A little way ahead of me, and closer to that left touchline, Cristiano Doni turned back onto his right foot and chipped a diagonal ball towards the goal. I watched for anything that might happen in the area, unconcerned about any possible offside. After all, I had a specialist assistant referee to do that, and I was happy to leave offside to him.

As Doni's lofted pass reached the six-yard box, Gianluca Zambrotta made a run towards the near post, jumped acrobatically, stuck out his right foot while in mid-air and flicked the ball across the goal to the far post. Christian Vieri, the big, bull-necked striker, dived and headed the ball home. It looked like a good goal for Italy. But Larsen stuck up his flag.

He stood there, in the correct and classic assistant's pose, square on to the pitch, feet apart, flag held straight out in front of him in his right hand. Fair enough, I thought, and disallowed the goal. Vieri looked across at Larsen and pointed down at his chest with a wide-eyed look on his face, as if to ask, 'Me?' Larsen nodded to indicate, 'Yes, you.'

The Italians protested strongly, and I had to book Vieri for dissent when he made a series of gestures at Larsen. If you watch Mafia movies, you will know the sort I mean. Yet all that was normal enough after a disallowed goal and I had no particular reason to doubt my assistant. Even if he had got it wrong, I thought to myself, it was probably a marginal decision, and I certainly could not over-rule him, because I had been in no position to see whether he was right or not.

Vieri struck again five minutes later with another header. This time Larsen was happy, and so I signalled a goal. Everything still seemed relatively straightforward. As Croatia staged an epic fight-back to take the lead with goals from Ivica Olic and Milan Rapaic, I had no sense at all that things had already gone calamitously awry for me.

Then, in stoppage time, I awarded the Italians a free-kick deep in their own half and made sure they took it from the correct place. The ball was knocked a short way forward to Marco Materazzi (whom we met in Chapter Two). The tall, well-built defender strode into the centre circle and then, still in his own half, hoofed the ball forward, left-footed, straight up the middle of the pitch. It soared like a golf ball sailing imperiously up the fairway, bounced once just short of the penalty spot and then bounced again a little further forward. As striker Filippo Inzaghi and goalkeeper Stipe Pletikosa converged on it, the ball eluded them both. It bobbled on undisturbed and slowly completed its progress into the net.

Larsen stuck his flag up again. This time he had it in his left hand and it was pointing down the touchline towards the Italian half. He wanted a free-kick to Croatia. With his right hand he made a tugging motion to indicate that he had seen a shirt-pull. I learned later that he claimed to have seen Inzaghi yank the shirt of Simunic – the man to whom I showed three yellow cards in the 2006 World Cup.

Spooky though that coincidence seems to me now, back in 2002, of course, the name Simunic meant nothing to me. As for Larsen's flag, I didn't know what he'd seen but I realized that I had to accept his decision. I was a long way away – too far, I concede, because I had been fussing over the placing of the ball for the free-kick. Though I had made some progress up the pitch as the kick was taken and as Materazzi pumped the ball forward, when it arrived in the area I was still only midway in the Croatian half. If Larsen had seen a shirt-tug, then I could not argue. But I knew there would be uproar, because the decision condemned Italy to defeat. Sure enough, at the finish, I was surrounded by extremely unhappy Italians.

As soon as Alarcon arrived in the referee's room after the game, he told us that it had been a terrible mistake to disallow the first goal for offside. Alarcon had seen replays on television. The following afternoon, at the debrief, I saw replays for myself and agreed that the decision was a howler. In fact, the entire room agreed. When the ball was played into the box by Doni, Vieri was about two yards onside. Zambrotta was a fraction further forward, but also clearly onside. Both Zambrotta and Vieri timed their runs perfectly as the ball reached the six-yard box, and when Zambrotta flicked the ball on, Vieri was behind the ball and, at worst, level with the last outfield defender. It was an utterly incomprehensible decision to rule Vieri offside.

It was that element – the bewildering ineptitude of the decision – that made it so controversial. I certainly did not suspect Larsen of being in any way part of some sort of corruption. Yet in the following days, weeks and months a sequence of events unfolded that convinced the Italians that disallowing the Vieri goal, along with the later long-range Matterazi effort, was part of a plot against them.

On 13 June, in Ōita, Italy played their final group match, against Mexico. The referee was Carlos Eugênio Simon of Brazil. Italy had two goals disallowed for offside, one in each half. The first was an Inzaghi 'goal', and replays showed that the offside ruling by assistant referee Mat Lazim Awang Hamat of Malaysia looked mistaken. The second disallowed 'goal' came from Vincenzo Montella, and this time it was the other assistant, Brazilian Jorge Oliveira, who raised his flag to signal the offence. Replays suggest that the officials got that one right. The match ended 1–1.

Five days later, Italy faced South Korea in a 'round of sixteen' match in Rifu. The referee, Byron Moreno of Ecuador, awarded the Koreans a hotly disputed penalty, which they failed to convert. The Italians then suffered another questionable offside decision when Moreno disallowed a Damiano Tomassi goal that would have won the game. Next, the ref sent off striker Francesco Totti in extra-time for a second yellow card offence: diving. Replays showed that he had been fouled. Eventually, Italy lost 2–1.

Three months later the Ecuadorian Football Federation suspended referee Moreno for 20 matches for 'unethical behaviour' at a league match.

Now you can see the continuum of events that began at my match. The Italians had five goals disallowed in three matches, were eliminated from the World Cup in a highly contentious game, and then the ref in charge of that fixture was charged and found guilty by his own Federation of being unethical – and I found myself slap-bang in the middle of a conspiracy theory.

THE ISSUES

The complaints about my match began as soon as it ended, long before Italian suspicions were raised about any other games or circumstances. The Italians felt grievously hard done by. They insisted that if both disallowed goals had been permitted to stand, they would have won. That is a flawed claim, because there is no way of knowing what would have happened if the first 'offside' effort had been allowed – Italy did take the lead soon afterwards anyway. The stoppage time 'goal', which Larsen struck off for shirt pulling, would only have given Italy a draw – and a point would have made no difference at all to their eventual second place finish in their group.

The game made a difference to *me*, however. It was Larsen who had erred, but FIFA's director of refereeing, Scotsman George Cumming, told me afterwards, 'Unfortunately the referee takes responsibility for what happens during a game. You can have no more games at this World Cup.'

I wanted to go home straightaway and be with my wife Julia and the children in Tring. FIFA wanted me to stay on until the official cull took place of refs and assistants who were not required for the later stages of the tournament. I remembered what Paul Durkin had told me about his poor reaction to disappointment in 1998. It was hard, but I persuaded myself to stay, keep training with everyone else, put on a forced smile and pretend that I was not devastated. That response pleased FIFA, and I was given one more appointment: Fourth Official to Collina at the last-sixteen match in which Turkey beat Japan 1–0 on 18 June in Rifu.

That match was in the afternoon. The Italy–South Korea fixture kicked off five hours later, in the evening of the same day, and the Italians believed Moreno favoured the Koreans throughout. They were convinced he had been got at.

Because Japan had been knocked out that afternoon, it was suggested that FIFA were desperate for the other co-hosts, the South Koreans, to stay in the tournament. At least one of the host nations needed to retain an interest in the tournament, so the argument went. Italian players, officials and journalists alleged openly that the referee had been instructed to secure a Korean victory. Totti, the player sent off, said, 'It was a scandal. This was a desired elimination. There are things greater than me but the feeling is that they wanted us out.'

FIFA were bullish in their denials and their support for Moreno. When he returned home, he also had the support of his fellow countrymen. In fact, he received a standing ovation from the crowd at his first game back. Perhaps encouraged by such unusual acclaim for a referee, Moreno announced that he was standing for election to the city council of Quito. He hoped to represent a district called Ponceano. With the poll pending, he took charge of a league game involving one of the Quito clubs: Liga Deportiva Universitaria, many of whose supporters live in Ponceano. They played Barcelona Sporting Club from Guayaquil. After 90 minutes, the Quito team trailed 3–2. Moreno said there would be 6 minutes of added time but actually allowed 13, during which the Quito team scored twice to win the match. The Barcelona president said it was unethical for an election candidate to referee matches involving a club supported by people from the area he hoped to represent.

An inquiry revealed that the goal times recorded in Moreno's official match report were inaccurate; all were shown as having been scored within the first 90 minutes. The Ecuadorian Federation suspended Moreno for 20 games.

In his third game after the suspension ended, he refereed another Quito team, Deportivo, and sent off three of their players. Deportivo are big rivals of Liga Deportiva Universitaria. Moreno was suspended again, this time for only one match. He retired soon afterwards, but FIFA, egged on by the Italians, launched an inquiry into Moreno, promising to include his handling of the Italy–South Korea match at the World Cup. The inquiry lasted four months before FIFA finally announced they could find no evidence of any wrongdoing and were 'closing the book' on Moreno without imposing any sanctions against him.

Italians had long since come to their own judgement and in Sicily a row of new public toilets was named after him. Oh, and he lost the election in Quito.

So the single issue that dominated the 2002 World Cup was the refereeing. It was generally agreed that it wasn't very good, but was it corrupt? Was there a conspiracy against the Italians? Or were they victims of a decision aimed at ensuring the hosts progressed?

I can speak definitively about myself and the game I refereed. I assert categorically that there was no Machiavellian plot involved, just mistakes by an assistant who was under pressure to 'be strong'. The game took place long before anyone knew whether Japan or South Korea or both would survive the group stages and so that was certainly not a factor. And in all the intervening years, nobody has ever been able to explain to me why I or anyone else might want Italy to be beaten by Croatia.

As a last argument for my defence, consider this: if there was some dark plot against Italy involving referees, assistants and FIFA officials, why was I told I could not referee any more games in that World Cup after taking charge of a game in which Italy lost?

Similarly, we can discount the idea that there was a plot against the Italians in their match against Mexico. Such a claim involves unsustainable assumptions. The conspiracy would have had to involve two Brazilians and a Malaysian (the match officials) and a room full of high-ranking FIFA dignitaries of various nationalities.

It is not so easy to exonerate Moreno, and the events in Ecuador when he went home undermined the credibility of all referees. But there are two possible explanations for his refereeing at the World Cup that do not involve corruption or collusion. One is that he just had a bad day and made a lot of honest mistakes. The other is that he got some things right and some wrong – as we all do when we referee – but that the Italians were convinced there was skullduggery because they were used to intrigue and scandal.

There have been a number of proven cases of match-fixing in Italian football, often involving referees. In 1980, for instance, AC Milan and Lazio were relegated from the top division and there were another two cases soon after the 2002 World Cup. In 2005 Genoa were relegated to the third division and, in May 2006, police intercepted telephone conversations that indicated several top clubs were trying to rig results by making sure matches were refereed by 'favourable' officials. I was caught up in the 2006 scandal because it involved taped telephone conversations made over several months and, in one of them, one of the accused men said he did not want me in charge of a Champions League game. He wanted someone else.

What happened was that Juventus drew 2–2 at home to Djurgarden of Sweden in the first leg of the third qualifying round of the Champions League on 10 August 2005. On the same night, I refereed Basel of Switzerland against Inter Milan. The normal procedure was for officials to be given one match each round, either a first or second leg. So I made my way home from Switzerland and was surprised later to receive another call telling me I had also been given a second-leg match. I was a late call-up, a replacement, to take charge of Djurgarden against Juventus in Stockholm.

When all the wire-tap transcripts were produced during the corruption trials, one included Juventus director Luciano Moggi being told, two days before the match in Stockholm, that instead of the referee he'd been expecting, I had been given the game. Moggi then telephoned Pierluigi Pairetto, the Italian ex-referee who was vice-chairman of UEFA's referees' committee. The conversation between Moggi and Pairetto was also taped, and in it Pairetto said that something must have happened at the last minute for me to be given the game. I don't know what that something was, but on 25 August 2005 I took charge of Djurgarden against Juventus. The Italians won 4–1 for a 6–3 aggregate win.

During the corruption trials, it was claimed that on one occasion Moggi sometimes arranged favours for people who had helped him. It was alleged that he helped one person jump the waiting list for a Maserati sports car. I should point out that I drive a Saab, and that I did not pick it up in Stockholm that night! I did not have any conversations which made me suspicious about the match itself, and certainly did nothing deliberate to influence the result.

In July 2006, in the week after Italy won the World Cup, Moggi received a suspended prison sentence and was banned from football for five years. Pairetto, who had refereed the Euro 96 final at Wembley in which Germany beat the Czech Republic, was banned for three and a half years. Juventus were relegated to Serie B. That was all four years after assistant referee Larsen stuck up his flag to infuriate the Italians, but it is possible that the waters were already murky in 2002 and that the Italians believed other countries and other officials might well be stained.

Also, in the build-up to the 2002 World Cup, there were allegations of promises being made and favours offered in two campaigns to secure votes. One was the bidding process for the right to host the 2006 World Cup (the vote for which was in 2000). The other was the contested re-election of Sepp Blatter as FIFA president, which occurred in May 2002, just before the World Cup.

The 2006 campaigners denied any wrongdoing. So did Blatter and his opponent, Issa Hayatou. I am certainly not alleging corruption, but there were so many accusations flying around when the 72 officials (36 refs and 36 assistants) arrived at the 2002 World Cup that there was a feeling of unease among us all. I put it no stronger than that.

In the small hours of the morning before the match I refereed, I was woken up by something being pushed under the door of my hotel room. It was a large brown envelope. It contained good luck cards and messages from family and friends that had been passed on to Phil Sharp, the English assistant, for him to give to me. But I did wonder briefly, as I got up to have a look, whether it was stuffed with money.

In that climate, I am not surprised the Italians suspected Moreno. I can even understand why they had their doubts about my match – and although I had no knowledge of any conspiracy theories at the time of the Italy–Croatia game, I was certainly fully aware of them by the time I flew home. I walked across the departure lounge at Tokyo's Narita airport carrying over $22,000 in the inside pocket of my FIFA blazer. Like all the match officials, I had been paid my attendance fee and expenses in cash. I felt very uncomfortable and am glad nobody asked me to explain why I had all those readies.

THE REF'S DECISION

Now, looking back down the years, I still feel my treatment at the 2002 World Cup was an injustice. My chance of refereeing more than one game was ended without my making a significant mistake. I could not go against Larsen's offside decision, and his shirt-tugging ruling was, at worst, debatable. There had been a bit of pulling and pushing from both sets of players but nobody could really argue that Larsen was wrong. My crime was that I had been too far away to make my own judgement – but my real crime, for both disallowed goals, was that the Italians were involved. They were and are a major footballing power, and FIFA could not tolerate blunders or even perceived blunders against them – not least because they always kicked up such a fuss.

But then FIFA create their own fuss whenever a big team lose unexpectedly. The game is analysed more carefully, and the debrief of the referee is more thorough and often more critical. FIFA would say they are protecting the integrity of football by ensuring, in the event of a surprise result, that it was not due to anything untoward. Conspiracy theorists speculate that, because the major football nations generate the biggest TV fees, FIFA have a commercial incentive to ensure those nations stay in tournaments as long as possible. I would argue that human nature is operating: a surprise result always attracts more attention.

Whatever the cause, or combination of causes, the effect is to make referees realize that they will come under enhanced scrutiny if a major nation loses. The best referees do not let that realization influence them. But not everyone is able to perform that trick of the mind.

Acknowledging such pressure is not the same as suggesting there has ever been a conspiracy to favour certain teams in World Cups. All I can say is that nobody has ever remarked to me, or even implied with a nod and a wink, that a particular result would be well received.

As far as the specific accusations are concerned about FIFA favouring the host nations in 2002, is it really so surprising that Japan and South Korea did well on their own territory? After all, there are plenty of teams who have punched above their weight in World Cups and both host countries in 2002 were meticulous in their preparations. Their players had focused on the tournament for years. Remember also that the Koreans were coached by Guus Hiddink, who had further World Cup success with Australia four years later before taking charge of Russia.

What we *can* conclude, both from my fixture at the 2002 World Cup and other games in which goals were disallowed, is that we have to simplify the offside law. Despite what some TV pundits tell you, the Law at present is not difficult to grasp, yet you will still see assistant referees making mistakes, because they have too many judgements to make, too many 'what ifs' to ponder.

I have two alternative Laws to propose, and would like to see experiments in either or both.

One is to scrap offside entirely. Nobody would be offside in any circumstances. That would probably lead to at least one striker 'goal-hanging' at each end, but would that be such a bad thing? I have talked the idea over with Sir Alex Ferguson and he says that if the opposition stationed a striker in the Manchester United penalty area (and that player could not be offside) then United would have to decide whether to leave a man back to mark him – and they probably would. That would stretch the play out and make the midfield less packed.

There would certainly be a refereeing advantage because, if the assistants did not have to think about offside, they could take very different positions on the touchlines. They would not have to do that manic little sideways dance as they try to keep level with the last outfield defender. Yes, they would still have to decide when the ball goes out of play and so forth, but they would be able to take up positions offering a better view of the action. The referee would have the help of two extra sets of eyes.

A definite downside of my proposal is that it would do away with one of the game's great skills – the perfectly timed run by a striker moving on to a slide-rule pass. So my second idea is to keep the offside Law for part of the pitch. I'd like to see, as an experiment, a change in the Law so that you can only be offside in the last 18 yards of each half. I say 18, because that is the depth of the penalty area. I'd extend the line at the front edge of each penalty area and make it run completely across the pitch, from sideline to sideline. Ahead of that line would be the part of the pitch in which the offside Law applies. But you couldn't be offside in the band of the pitch between the halfway line and the new, 18-yard line.

I would then simplify the interpretation and merely say that being in an offside position when the ball is played forward is an offence. In other words, if you are standing offside in the final 18 yards of the pitch, when the ball is played forward, you are offside. In the rest of the half, you are not.

You would still have players making clever runs and so on at the business ends of the pitch, but you would stop the infuriating incidents in which players are judged offside just a stride or two over the halfway line. This idea is an adaptation of one tried in England in the 1971/72 season in a competition called the Watney Cup. As an experiment, it was decreed that a player could only be offside in the opponents' penalty area. An official report on the trial was very positive. Then they did nothing about it.

Interestingly, hockey (the version not played on ice) changed the offside law several times. Initially a player was in an offside position if he had fewer than three opponents between him and the goal. In 1972 that was reduced to two defenders. In 1987 it was changed so that you were only offside in the final 25 yards of the pitch. In 1996 a 'mandatory experiment' was introduced in which offside was scrapped completely. And two years later that experiment became law – and nobody has had to worry about offside ever since. I speak to a lot of mates who play hockey, and they all say that the game is better now because doing away with offside has ended all the ambiguity and uncertainty.

Perhaps my two ideas would prove to be poor or bad for the game of football, but we cannot know unless we experiment, and we have to do something to make the Law simpler – not easier to understand but more straightforward to apply. It is easy enough to explain and understand the offside Law, but it is impossible to adjudicate accurately, consistently and fairly. A Law that is so frequently misapplied is a bad Law.

WORLD CUP STATS: 2002

QUALIFICATION TOURNAMENT: Because, for the first tournament in World Cup history, the finals were to be hosted by two countries, three nations automatically qualified – hosts Japan and South Korea, plus defending champions France. There were 29 other places at stake. All seven previous World Cup-winning nations (Argentina, Brazil, England, France, Germany, Italy and Uruguay) qualified. Kevin Keegan resigned as England manager immediately after the qualifying group-match defeat by Germany (the last competitive match at Wembley before the old stadium was demolished). He was replaced by Sven-Goran Eriksson who oversaw a 5–1 victory over the Germans in Munich and achieved qualification in the final fixture when David Beckham scored with a last-gasp free-kick against Greece at Old Trafford. None of the other home countries qualified. Scotland lost only one of their qualifying matches but finished third in their group behind Croatia and Belgium. Wales won only once and finished fifth out of six, above only Armenia. Northern Ireland also finished fifth of six (above Malta) but managed three wins and two draws in their ten games.

FINALS: 31 May to 30 June. Thirty-two teams from five federations

HOSTS: Japan and South Korea

MASCOT: Ato, Kaz and Nik (alien creatures known collectively as 'The Spheriks')

FINAL: Brazil 2, Germany 0

MATCHES PLAYED: 64

GOALS SCORED: 161

ATTENDANCE: 2,705,197

TOP SCORER: Ronaldo (Brazil, 8 goals)

BEST PLAYER: Oliver Kahn (Germany)

HOME NATIONS: England's build-up to the tournament was dominated by almost daily bulletins about David Beckham's chances of recovering from a broken bone in his foot. He did, and played in every England fixture in Japan, but was short of fitness and seemingly reluctant to use his damaged right foot. England, managed by Sven-Goran Eriksson, drew with Sweden and then beat Argentina (Beckham, sent off when the teams met at France in the 1998 World Cup, scored the only goal from the penalty spot). But then England drew with

Nigeria and finished second in their group. England beat Denmark in the 'round of sixteen' and then met Brazil in the quarter-final. Michael Owen gave England the lead but Brazil were level by half-time through Rivaldo. Then a 40-yard free-kick by Ronaldinho caught goalkeeper David Seaman off his line and gave Brazil the lead – which they held on to, despite having Ronaldinho sent off with 33 minutes still to play. Brazil went on to win the tournament.

PEERLESS PIERLUIGI

Pierluigi Collina, the best referee of my generation, had the room next to me at our 2002 base in Japan. He missed the debriefing for my Italy–Croatia match because he was away from our training camp at a match. But he watched the video of the key incidents later and made a very good point to me privately. Immediately before the second disallowed Italian goal, I had made sure that they placed the ball absolutely correctly for a free-kick in their own half. Collina said to me, 'I do not understand why you prioritized the positioning of the football in an innocuous position. There were not many seconds left. Italy wanted a goal. It was obvious that the Italians would send the ball into the Croatia penalty area. Your attention was needed where the ball was going.' Collina, who was always meticulous in his preparation and planning, would have left nothing to chance in the last moments of the Italy–Croatia game. Unfortunately, I did.

OFF, OFF, OFF

THE term 'offside' is used by several sports. Rugby Union's offside law is more complex than football's, for instance, and you can also be offside in ice hockey.

The word 'offside' derived from a 19th-century military term 'off the strength of his side'. When a soldier was 'on the strength of his unit' or 'on the strength of his side' he was entitled to the appropriate pay and rations. If, for some reason, he was off the strength of his unit or side he had no such entitlement.

When ball sports were first given different sets of rules at several public schools, forward passing was banned, and so players were said to be 'off their side' if they were ahead of the ball because they could not join in. The phrase was shortened, over time, to 'off-side' and then to 'offside'.

Not a lot of people know that.

And I don't think a lot of people have thought of this: why do we still have a Law which derives from the fact that you used not to be allowed to pass forwards? The forward-pass ban has been enshrined in rugby, but has no place in football, so why do we still worry about offside? All the other Laws of football have an obvious purpose. Kicking people is wrong, for instance, and you can see the sense of giving a corner if a defender kicks the ball over his own goal-line. But there is no longer any inherent reason for saying it is wrong to be 'off the strength' in football.

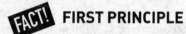 **FIRST PRINCIPLE**

LAW Eleven deals with offside and the very first sentence says, 'It is not an offence in itself to be in an offside position.' That is the key principle. A player standing (or even running about) in an offside position is not necessarily committing an offence, and so the assistant referee will not necessarily flag.

The next bit of the Law says, 'A player is in an offside position if he is nearer to his opponent's goal-line than both the ball and the second last opponent.' That is straightforward enough, isn't it? It means that the assistant must look to see whether there are two opponents between the attacker and the goal-line, although one of them is usually (but not necessarily) the goalkeeper.

Right, we know what an offside position is. We know that being in that position is not necessarily an offence. So when does it become an offence? The Law says,

A player in an offside position is only penalised if, at the moment the ball touches or is played by one of his team, he is, in the opinion of the referee, involved in active play by

- interfering with play or
- interfering with an opponent or
- gaining an advantage by being in that position.

The Law then goes on to explain that you cannot be offside from a goal-kick, a throw-in or a corner.

ACTIVE INGREDIENT

One source of unnecessary confusion is that 'experts' on TV and radio use the dictionary definitions of some of the words and phrases in the Law, or invent their own. The correct thing to do would be to use the Law's definitions and FIFA's guidelines.

According to the Law, a player must be 'involved in active play' to be offside and any one of three things can make him active.

The first is 'interfering with play'. FIFA says a player is only 'interfering with play' if he is touching the ball. Even attempting to touch the ball does not count. Standing next to the ball does not count. Being in the vague vicinity of the ball definitely does not count. You have to touch it. Very few players, managers, pundits and supporters know that strict definition of 'interfering with play' and yet it has been the published guideline since 2005.

The second thing that makes a player active is 'interfering with an opponent'. That is not some allegation of improper behaviour. The guideline says it means interfering with an opponent's ability to play the ball by obstructing the opponent's line of vision, blocking the opponent's movement, or making a gesture or movement which distracts the opponent.

Finally, the third thing that makes a player active is if he gains an advantage from being in an offside position. Again, the guideline is specific and restrictive and the definition of gaining an advantage is far, far narrower than many players, managers, journalists and fans understand. It states that a player in an offside position only gains an advantage by playing a ball that rebounds to him from an opponent, the post or the crossbar.

The thinking there is simple. If you are offside when someone shoots and the ball hits the bar, the goalkeeper or a defender on the line and rebounds straight to you, you are no longer offside (because the ball is in front of you). But you have gained such a huge advantage by your earlier offside position that you should be penalized. But nothing else counts as 'gaining an advantage'.

If you are standing in an offside position in the middle of the penalty area and the ball is played out to your winger, you are not penalized, because you haven't fulfilled any of the three criteria for being actively involved in play. Then, if the winger gets to the byline and cuts the ball back to you, you are no longer in an offside position (because the ball is in front of you). Play has moved on into a different phase, and you are not penalized for 'gaining an advantage' from your earlier offside position.

The idea of phases of play confuses some people, but it is not a difficult concept and it is not crucial to your understanding of offside.

The other thing to remember is Law Eighteen – the one that doesn't exist but every ref knows about. It says you should use common sense. So, if a player in an offside position chases after the ball and is clearly going to get to it, you don't have to wait for him to touch it to give him offside.

The offside Law isn't difficult really, is it? Yet, week after week, television 'experts' tell you that it is. They are mostly old defenders who hanker after the days when they could just step forward and stick their hands up. They choose not to accept the new interpretations. If I sit down and explain the new interpretation to someone who played in the old era, he will usually say, 'That's wrong'. They deliberately refuse to accept the Law as it is now applied.

THE FULL ARSENAL

When I played football, and for many years after I began refereeing, the first principle of offside (that it is not an offence merely to be in an offside position) was ignored. If you were standing in an offside position, you were offside. The idea that someone might not be active was dismissed by Liverpool manager Bill Shankly. He said, 'What is he doing on the pitch then?'

Teams became adept at catching opponents offside. The defence used to step forward in unison and leave a striker stranded behind them. One or more defenders would then stick up their arms to appeal and applaud the 'lino' when he obliged by putting up his flag. The most proficient exponents of this offside 'trap' were Arsenal, whose synchronized routine – step forward, arm up – was parodied in the film The Full Monty, in which a group of unemployed steelworkers were learning to dance for a striptease act.

But the offside trap led to sterile games, when attack after attack was thwarted far too easily, although the number of goals at World Cups did not decline as much as is sometimes suggested. In 1970 there were on average 2.97 goals per game. In the 2002 finals, the average had only slipped to 2.52 per game. Nonetheless, there was a general feeling within FIFA that the trend was towards better organized defences and less exciting matches. It was decided that attackers should be given some help by making match officials apply the offside Law's first principle.

RED CARD FOR COMMENTATORS

TWO myths about assistant referees are perpetuated by ignorant commentators. One is that an assistant who waits until an offside player becomes active before flagging is slow or not concentrating. Usually he signals as soon as the offence is committed. Yet in most match commentaries you will hear a broadcaster saying, 'That was a very late flag.'

The other myth is that an assistant should signal whenever he sees a foul. That is not true. Let me elaborate by explaining how, when I was refereeing, I expected assistants to respond if there was a potential penalty.

If there was a foul or handball in the area, and it was possibly a penalty, then I wanted the assistant's first instinct to be to look at me. If I had seen the incident and was pointing to the spot, then the assistant had nothing to do. If I had seen the incident and was signalling, 'No!', then

I did not want the assistant to contradict me by signalling a penalty. The third possibility was that I did not have a good view of the incident. I would then look over to the assistant and, by doing so, invite him to get involved. An invitation should always elicit a response, and in this case I expected the assistant either to signal for a penalty (by putting his flag across his chest, pointing towards the goal-line) or to indicate it was not a penalty (by inverting his flag, using some predetermined hand-signal or shaking his head). Of course, once lip microphones and earpieces were introduced, we could just talk to each other, but the principle was the same. It was the referee's duty and responsibility to decide about penalties, and only a task for the assistant if an invitation to do so was extended to him.

OFF THEIR TROLLEYS

The suggestion that referees might be open to bribes is a serious one, and so I was always careful about accepting gifts from clubs I refereed. That didn't mean I didn't take any – I was just careful what I chose!

There were potential pitfalls, especially in my early days on the FIFA list, when officials were not paid match fees and so it was considered entirely proper by most clubs to provide some recompense by means of a gift. I was given a stereo in Belgium, several watches from trips to Spain and so on.

The problem with that was that rich clubs could afford more expensive gifts, and poorer clubs felt refs might favour those who showered them with luxury items.

There was also an understanding at many clubs that refs would help themselves to anything they fancied at the club shop and not have to pay. At Borussia Dortmund they used to give you a trolley, and for some officials it was like playing *Supermarket Sweep*.

If my officials and I were invited to help ourselves in the club shop, I used to say to the assistants and Fourth Official, 'Each choose two items maximum lads.' It felt wrong to take more than, say, a replica shirt and a pin badge, and I certainly did not want representatives of the visiting club to see the ref and his team leaving the shop laden down with goodies.

English clubs never really went in for the idea of giving expensive gifts to refs. There was just a different culture at our clubs. If visiting match officials said something like, 'Can we go to the club shop?', the English club might just about let them have staff discount. There were seldom any freebies.

That helped emphasize the feeling that the English were neither corrupt nor corruptible – and that belief extended to the way referees were regarded. It is still the case that the rest of the world believes our referees are entirely honourable and I believe the assessment is fully justified.

10

MY GERMAN LESSON

THE MATCH

The 2006 World Cup was a great success for the hosts, Germany. They did not win the tournament – they finished third – but the part they played in the organization was hailed as a triumph, particularly the 'fan zones' in city centres throughout the country, where big crowds watched the matches on giant screens with a maximum amount of passion (plus a considerable amount of beer) and yet a minimum amount of trouble.

The 2006 World Cup did not go as well for the English. The national team arrived with the usual hugely over-hyped expectations and left with the familiar crushed sense of anti-climax after losing in a penalty shoot-out in the quarter-finals (again!). Things did not go well, either, for the English referee: G. Poll, from Tring in Hertfordshire (again!).

I took charge of three matches. Appropriately enough, I made my famous mistake for which I am remembered in the third. I was wearing my third differently coloured referee's shirt of the tournament. The game was in my third different city, and my third different group. It was the third match for each of the teams and the mistake involved a player wearing the number three. In case you are wondering, three is not my lucky number.

It all happened on Thursday 22 June 2006, in Stuttgart, in the Group F match between Croatia and Australia.

Croatia were only able to enter the World Cup from the 1998 tournament onwards, and had qualified for the finals every time since. The Australians, known as the Socceroos, were competing in their first World Cup finals tournament for 32 years.

In Germany, Australia beat Japan but lost to World Champions Brazil. Croatia lost to Brazil and then drew with Japan. So, by the time the Socceroos and Croatians met in Stuttgart, the Aussies knew that they had only to avoid defeat to go through to the 'round of sixteen' as runners-up behind group winners Brazil. But a win for Croatia would carry them through. One television commentary began with the words, 'It's do or die in Stuttgart.'

Just three minutes into the game, Darijo Srna gave Croatia the lead from a free-kick after Mark Viduka (who has played for Celtic, Leeds, Middlesbrough and Newcastle) brought down Niko Kovac. Australia equalized six minutes before half-time with a penalty – and I was pleased about the decisions that led to both goals.

For the first, I could have allowed play to continue, because Croatia kept possession after the foul, but my instinct was that giving them a free-kick 28 yards out was better than allowing the advantage. Srna's excellent execution of his free-kick justified that instinct.

His right-footed, curling shot flew over the defensive wall and tucked just inside the left-hand post.

For the equalizer, I silently congratulated myself on a good spot when I noticed Stjepan Thomas handling the ball in the penalty area. The penalty was drilled home by Craig Moore, who played for Glasgow Rangers and Newcastle.

Croatia needed to win, remember, and Australia only required a draw. So you can imagine the contrasting emotions among the rival supporters in the 52,000 crowd when, after 56 minutes, Socceroos' goalkeeper Zeljko Kalac made a terrible blunder and allowed Kovac's 30-yard drive to evade him and bobble into the net. It was 2–1 to Croatia.

Six minutes later, Josep Simunic body-checked Australia's Harry Kewell (formerly of Leeds and then of Liverpool). I showed the Croat a yellow card and recorded the caution in my notebook – exactly as I had noted bookings in the previous 1,499 games I had refereed. I always identified teams in my notebook by their colours rather than their names. The reasoning was that if, for instance, I put 'Blue' for Everton and 'Red' for Arsenal, all I had to think about was the shirt colour of the player about whom I was making a note. So, for the Stuttgart game, I drew a line down a page of my notebook to divide the page into two vertical columns. I wrote 'Red/White' for Croatia at the top of the left-hand column and 'Yellow' for Australia on the right. Beneath each heading I listed the shirt-numbers of the players in each team. And so, after 61 minutes, I wrote 'C' for caution against Red/White number three in the left-hand column and noted the time: '16/2' (16 minutes of the second half).

Another 17 frenetic minutes passed. Then, Aussie substitute Mark Bresciano centred from the right and another sub, John Aloisi (Coventry and Portsmouth), nodded the ball on. Kewell, at the far post, took one touch to control the ball and scored with his second. It was 2–2. If it stayed like that, Australia would go through and Croatia would go home, so the final moments were incredibly exciting and tense.

I sent off Croatia's Dario Simic and Australia's Brett Emerton (Blackburn) in the last ten minutes, both for getting a second yellow card. I had recorded their first cautions correctly but I did not have to look them up. When Simic committed a bad foul, I knew he'd already had a yellow, so I got out the red. Again, when Emerton stopped an attack by handling the ball, I realized he'd had a yellow and I got out the red once more without checking my notebook or needing to.

Then, in stoppage time, I yellow-carded Simunic for fouling Australia sub Joshua Kennedy. It was Simunic's second yellow, but for some reason it just did not register. That was my first error, and another followed quickly. Assuming it was a first caution for Simunic, I recorded it in my notebook, but I inserted 'C' in the Yellow column, alongside the name of their number three. That was the Australia column.

Simunic was born in Australia. He grew up in Australia. He graduated from the Australian Institute of Sport. And although he played for Croatia, he has such a pronounced Australian accent that his nickname is 'Aussie Joe'. When I booked him the second time, he said, 'That's unbelievable', in his thick Aussie accent. So did I just think, subconsciously, that I was dealing with an Australian? Was that why I put 'C' in the Australian column? I don't know. I just know that the error changed my life.

If I had used the correct column, I would have spotted immediately that there was already a 'C' against the name of the Croatian number three. I would have sent off Simunic, and my life would have continued down a very different path.

At the time, however, I had no inkling of any major controversy as the match ended. I had given a total of eight yellows, two of which had led (correctly) to sendings off. It had been mayhem, but it had been an epic match. The Aussies celebrated. Some of the Croatians slumped onto their haunches and some of them were in tears.

Simunic did not weep. He strode towards me belligerently and gave me some verbals. I waved him away, but he followed me and continued to vent his frustration about Croatia's elimination on me. It was clear and excessive dissent, so I showed him the yellow card and, remembering the second of his two previous cautions (but not the first!), I fished in the breast pocket of my shirt and pulled out the red card.

We all left the field. Everywhere around the globe, television had highlighted the fact that I had shown Simunic three yellow cards. The world was discussing my 'three card trick'. But in the calm of the officials' dressing room, we had no idea that anything was amiss. We thought we'd done rather well.

I went along the corridor for a massage and it was while I was having the fatigue rubbed out of my legs that Eugene Striegel, a German refereeing administrator, entered the room.

He said, 'There is a problem'.

THE ISSUES

My blunder did not affect the result of the match. The score was 2–2 when I erroneously allowed Simunic to stay on the pitch after two cautions. The score was 2–2 at the finish.

But between my mistake and the final whistle, Croatia had mounted a sustained period of pressure as they hunted for the goal that would have carried them through to the next round. Luka Modric (later to join Tottenham) pinged in a decent shot and there had also been a corner. If Croatia had scored while Simunic was on the pitch illegally, FIFA would have replayed the game. FIFA had already set a precedent – and I knew all about it.

On 3 September 2005, in Tashkent, Uzbekistan played Bahrain in the first leg of a World Cup qualifying play-off. Uzbekistan were leading 1–0 when they were awarded a penalty. They scored, but Japanese referee Toshimitsu Yoshida disallowed the goal because another Uzbekistan player had encroached into the penalty area.

So here is a quick quiz: what should the referee have done next?

The answer, according to Law Fourteen, is that he should have made Uzbekistan retake the penalty. Instead, he gave a free-kick to Bahrain. The match finished 1–0 – but the winners, Uzbekistan, protested. They argued that if the penalty had been retaken, they would probably have secured a two-goal lead for the second leg.

FIFA upheld their protest and ordered that the first leg should be replayed in its entirety. So the teams met again in Tashkent on 8 October and this time drew 1–1. The second leg was four days later in Bahrain, and I was the referee. I considered my appointment as a sign that FIFA placed great trust in me, because they were desperate that nothing should go wrong after the problem with the first match, and on the morning of my game in Bahrain I was telephoned five times by anxious FIFA administrators who wanted to go through the details with me.

In the event, the game ended 0–0 and so Bahrain went through on away goals. Uzbekistan might well have won the tie if they had accepted their 1–0 first-leg win – but, significantly, FIFA had established that a match in which the score might have been affected by a serious refereeing error should be replayed.

So, after my Stuttgart error, FIFA president Sepp Blatter said that if Australia had been eliminated from the tournament they would have had strong grounds for asking for the match with Croatia to be replayed – although scheduling an extra fixture would have wrecked the tournament.

Putting on a World Cup game is a huge logistical enterprise, involving tens of thousands of people. Roads are closed, hundreds of extra police are on duty, extra car-parks are arranged, along with special buses. Journalists and broadcasters, plus their technical staff, book their hotels and travel arrangements months in advance. Outside the stadium, the additional security involves erecting (and then later dismantling) miles of fencing to funnel spectators in different directions. Hundreds of specially trained security staff are on duty. Inside the stadium, there are far more staff than for an ordinary match.

The schedule of matches is arranged more than a year in advance, and all the requisite police, security, hotel staff, stadium staff – and so on and so on – are given their work rotas a long time before the match. If you suddenly say, 'Oh, we are going to put on an extra match in a couple of days' time', I'm not sure you could actually do it.

So my Stuttgart mistake could have caused chaos. I realized that immediately and was immensely relieved that no replay was required. But why did I make the mistake?

I had already refereed two matches at the 2006 finals before the Stuttgart fixture. My first was the opening game in Group G, South Korea against Togo (the 2002 semi-finalists against a nation that had never before been to the finals) in Frankfurt on Tuesday 13 June. I sent off Togo's Jean-Paul Abalo and the Koreans won 2–1. My second match was on Monday 19 June: Ukraine's 4–0 Group H romp against Saudi Arabia in slippery conditions in Hamburg.

There had been six days between those matches, which was about the norm for those refs at the 2006 World Cup who got more than one game. There was supposed to be plenty of time between fixtures, so that you could travel back to base, unwind, and then train and prepare properly for the next allotted appointment.

But, unexpectedly, the day after my Hamburg game, my name went up on the board for the Stuttgart fixture. I was elated because Croatia v Australia would be a real test, and I wanted to show FIFA I could pass that examination. The fact that there were only two clear days between the match days was a surprise, but not an issue.

In *Seeing Red*, I suggest that it became an issue. I speculate that I was too tired in Stuttgart. Certainly my mum, watching at home in England, said that I didn't look like myself. But I think that is looking for excuses. Yes, I was fatigued, and additionally I had picked up an injury during the game in Hamburg, but if either the tiredness or the pain in my back had been a problem then it was my responsibility to tell FIFA before going to Stuttgart.

The truth is, I don't think either was a problem. I'd had physio-therapy on my back, and the match schedule was not really daunt-ing. Almost every year when I refereed at the top of the domestic game in England, I had a match on Boxing Day, another two days' later on 28 December and then a third on New Year's Day. There was a similarly busy schedule every Easter. And the match officials at the 2006 World Cup were looked after very well. The physical preparation for matches was good, we had access to a sports psychologist and there was no reason at all why any of us should not have been able to perform in a series of matches in a relatively short space of time.

No, fatigue was not the reason I wrote 'C' in the wrong column.

But shouldn't the assistants and Fourth Official have stopped the error? In *Seeing Red* I explain in detail why I accept full responsibil-ity for what happened in Stuttgart. I have never sought to blame anyone else. I do not do so now. But on a more general refereeing point, then yes, the other match officials could and should have intervened.

My assistants in Stuttgart were my compatriots Phil Sharp and Glenn Turner. They should have been keeping their own record of cautions and when I showed the yellow card to Simunic the second time, one or both of the assistants should have spotted the error. They should have said, using the lip microphone, 'Pollie, you've already booked the Croatia number three.'

Even if they thought, 'I must be wrong; Pollie wouldn't make a mistake like that', they should still have intervened. One or other of them should have said, 'I need to check something before you proceed, Graham.' Neither said anything.

The Fourth Official was Kevin Stott, from the United States of America. As we have seen, the duties of the Fourth Official are very limited. They are set out on page 53 of FIFA's current Laws of the Game booklet. One of the bullet points begins, 'He must indicate to the referee when the wrong player is cautioned because of mistaken identity.'

That is what happened in Stuttgart. I recorded the identity of the wrong player. Stott is a good guy but, like the two assistants, he said nothing when I held up my yellow card to Simunic for a second time.

I repeat, the responsibility for what went wrong in Stuttgart on Thursday 22 June 2006 is mine. I made the error. But the silence of the rest of my 'team' in Stuttgart is an issue for football to worry about.

Three of us really were a team and had been for some while. Of the 56 or so matches I refereed in the 2005/06 season Sharp and Turner were my assistants in about 48 of them. I knew those guys really well. I knew their families. And those guys knew me – they could pick up my moods by nuances of body language, they knew my sense of humour, they knew about the long-term problem I'd had with my back, they knew the beliefs and philosophies by which I lived my life ... and they definitely knew every minute detail about how I refereed football matches.

So you can see how far the pendulum had swung in the 40 years since the events we looked at in Chapter One. On 30 July 1966, at the World Cup Final at Wembley, an Azerbaijani referee who was out of practice at running the line told a Swiss referee that Geoff Hurst's shot had crossed the goal-line. He did so by nodding his head, because the two officials did not have a common language. Fast forward to 22 June 2006 and running the line for the ref in Stuttgart were two men from his country – and not only were they specialist assistants, they were virtually specialists at assisting *him*.

The gradual changes which culminated in teams of officials taking charge of matches at the 2006 World Cup also eliminated the problem alluded to in Chapter Three – when the linesman, Bogdan Dotchev from Bulgaria, did not raise his flag when Diego Maradona 'scored' against England with help from 'the Hand of God'. Dotchev might well have resented (or at least not respected) the Tunisian referee, Ali Bennaceur. By 2006 those petty jealousies based on nationalities had been eradicated, because assistants were the same nationality as the ref.

The opposite problem – an assistant being in awe of a referee – was possible as recently as 2002. At that year's World Cup, when Italy's magnificent referee Pierluigi Collina took charge of England against Argentina in Sapporo (on 7 June), one of his assistants was Mohamed Saeed from the Maldives. I imagine Saeed was thinking two things. Firstly, 'There are more people in this stadium than live on my island.' Secondly, 'That is Pierluigi Collina!!!' I mean no disrespect to Saeed, but there is no way he would have queried any of Collina's judgements or rulings.

So by 2006, FIFA had dealt with the language problem, and with the potential problems of jealousies based on nationalities or of referees being awe-struck – yet there was obviously still a communication breakdown, because none of my team communicated anything to me about Simunic's second yellow card.

Perhaps the pendulum had swung too far. Perhaps Sharp and Turner knew me too well. They had been with me so often that I no longer bothered going through my instructions before every game. Perhaps, as a result, they'd switched on auto-pilot. Perhaps they did not think about what I wanted and what their duties were.

It has also been suggested to me that, although they were certainly not in awe of me, Sharp and Turner – and also Fourth Official Stott – trusted me too much. They assumed that I would not make a mistake like showing someone the yellow card twice without sending him off. Certainly my lovely wife Julia thought that. When television was dwelling on my 'three card trick' during coverage of the game in Stuttgart, she thought the commentators must be wrong. It couldn't be her husband. It couldn't be Graham Poll who was wrong. Well, now we all know that I was.

THE REF'S DECISION

I believe the lesson for match officials and for football itself from the silence of my assistants and the Fourth Official in Stuttgart is that assumption is the enemy of efficiency. Sharp, Turner and Stott were wrong to assume I could not make such a bad mistake. That assumption led them not to challenge me when I showed the yellow card to Simunic for the second time.

Yet their families were not subjected to the media intrusion that mine suffered.

The newspapers knew I was holed up in the referees' base near Frankfurt after my 'three card trick'. They knew because they were camped outside trying to get a picture of me looking broken. Meanwhile, their colleagues set up camp outside my family home in Tring as well. They wanted a photograph of my wife looking tearful or the chance to ask my young children what they thought of their dad's big blunder. I am not a footballer with a house behind big gates. I am just a referee, with a normal, vulnerable home. But those newspapers did not know that Julia was too strong to let them have the pleasure of seeing her unhappy and too smart to let them get near our children.

It still makes me angry to think about them camped outside our home in Tring while I was away halfway across Europe. Just as Graham Taylor was abused in 1993, so I think the media crossed the line between decency and depravity in 2006.

Another conclusion from the events that flowed from my mistake in 2006 parallels that which I drew from events surrounding Zinedine Zidane's head-butt in the Final (in Chapter Two). Just as I cannot believe FIFA will ever allow the possibility of someone going unpunished in a World Cup Final following an act of violence like that perpetrated by Zidane, so also I believe they will take steps to ensure that a referee never again brandishes a yellow card twice to the same player without producing the red.

I have no doubt they will stress to all officials the need to be pedantically correct with the formalities; to ensure the punctilious recording of cautions by the referee, both assistants and the Fourth Official. But I believe FIFA will go further than this. Just as I am convinced that, if necessary, they would make illicit use of TV monitors to make sure a head-butt is dealt with, so I am sure they would somehow get a message to the ref if he did the equivalent of a 'three card trick' and none of the other match officials spotted it.

To arrive at yet another conclusion from 2006, let me first tell you that, two months after the World Cup ended, something very disturbing happened in a less exalted competition: the Spartan South Midlands League.

Edgware Town were at home to Harefield United (on 5 September). The visitors were leading 1–0 when Edgware were given a penalty, which they tucked away. The referee, Mark Tweed, disallowed the goal for encroachment by an Edgware player and ... Have you guessed where this is going?

Tweed should have ordered the penalty to be retaken, but he gave Harefield a free-kick instead – exactly the mistake made by referee Yoshida in the Uzbekistan–Bahrain game. The Spartan South Midlands League reacted precisely as FIFA had in that case. When Edgware complained, the League ordered the match to be replayed.

I think FIFA and the Spartan South Midlands League were both dangerously misguided. If you accept their thinking then we could have dozens of games replayed every week, since beaten teams always blame the referee. And what if a team is relegated from the Premier League because, in the last game, the referee makes a mistake? Will the relegated club sue the ref, or the Premier League, for millions of pounds, citing the precedents of Yoshida and Tweed? That way lies Bedlam.

Yoshida and Tweed made mistakes, but, as I demonstrated in Stuttgart, all referees make mistakes. And that is my point. That is the point at the heart of this book.

We have used our time machine to discover why Gottfried Dienst and Tofik Bakhramov, the ref and linesman at Wembley in 1966, wrongly ruled that Geoff Hurst's shot had crossed the line. We have seen that, in the 2006 Final, referee Horacio Elizondo was not proactive enough to stop Zinedine Zidane head-butting an opponent and then missed the violent conduct when it occurred. Twenty years earlier, neither linesman Bogdan Dotchev nor referee Ali Bennaceur signalled for an infringement when Maradona scored with his hand. In 1982, Charles Corver allowed Harald Schumacher's 'crime of the century' to go unpunished. In 1978, Clive Thomas blew his whistle just as Brazil were scoring. In 1988, Kim Milton Nielsen should have treated David Beckham and Diego Simeone with parity. In the qualifying tournament for the 1994 World Cup, Karl-Josef Assenmacher should have sent off Ronald Koeman and so prevented him from scoring later against Graham Taylor's England. In 2002, assistant referee Jens Larsen made a spectacularly wrong call about an offside involving Italy.

And in Stuttgart on Thursday 22 June 2006, I should not have written the letter 'C' on the wrong side of a line in my notebook. I was a very good referee. FIFA recognized that. My CV demonstrated that. Yet in my 1500th match I made that error.

It was a moment's carelessness, but not the worst mistake that has occurred on a football field. I can think of plenty worse from every season. For instance, there was a shocker when Manchester United played Porto in the Champions League quarter-final first leg at Old Trafford on 7 April 2009. Porto centre-back Bruno Alves did not look up before striking a casual back-pass towards his goalkeeper, so he did not see Wayne Rooney. The pass went straight to Rooney, who scored. The following week, when Chelsea and Liverpool drew 4–4 in an absolutely epic quarter-final second leg at Stamford Bridge (14 April), both goalkeepers had a slipshod evening. Chelsea's Petr Cech got his positioning disastrously wrong and so Fabio Aurelio smashed a free-kick into the completely unguarded side of the net. Liverpool goalkeeper 'Pepe' Reina then scored an own goal when Didier Drogba's got a faint touch on a Nicolas Anelka cross and Reina spooned the ball into his own net.

Yet there were not newspaper people camped outside the homes of Alves, Cech and Reina, harassing their families. Ah, but they are footballers you see, not referees. It is referees who must not make mistakes. Only, of course, they always have and always will. No matter how much technology we use (even if we use it secretly), no matter how many procedures we improve, the game of football will always rely on men and women who are brave enough to put on referees' kits and go out and make honest, neutral decisions. They will make countless good, correct decisions. But occasionally they will get things wrong. To err is human. Get over it, and get on with the game.

A DATE WITH COINCIDENCE

Welsh referee Clive Thomas made his mark at the 1978 World Cup finals, as we saw in Chapter Five. He also had a remarkable and controversial impact four years earlier in the 1974 World Cup in Germany.

He was reserve official for a first-round match between Australia and Chile but all that the job was supposed to involve was sitting by the side of the pitch in a tracksuit in case someone was injured.

The referee, an Iranian called Jafar Namdar, cautioned Australia's Ray Richards in the first half, and then yellow-carded him again ten minutes from the end of the match – but did not send him off. The score was 0–0 and both teams were already on their way out of the tournament, so perhaps most people were not concerned about the error.

Richards remained on the pitch until Thomas could contain himself no longer. He got up and told a FIFA official about Richards and eventually the message reached the referee. Belatedly, the ref showed Richards the red card.

Thomas's intervention is interesting enough, confirming as it does my view that people are prepared to bend the rules to make sure that natural justice is served during a match. Thomas was not supposed to play any part in proceedings, but effectively he became an unofficial Fourth Official.

Here's one other aspect of the story that is intriguing: the date of the match was 22 June.

So on 22 June, in Germany, at a World Cup, in a match involving Australia, a referee showed his yellow card twice to the same player without sending him off. Thirty-two years later, on the same date, in a World Cup match in Germany involving Australia, I did the same thing.

PANEL GAMES

Replaying matches after a refereeing mistake is a recipe for chaos and demonstrates how far we have come from the idea that the referee is always right. Further proof is provided by the English system of reviewing red cards.

The idea is that, if a player thinks he has been wrongly sent off, an appeal panel is convened. In theory, the panel can only rescind the red card if the ref has made an error in law or obviously misinterpreted events. That is the theory, but what started to happen in the 2008/09 season was that the panels (which often did not include anyone who had ever refereed, by the way) started routinely overturning sendings off.

On 14 March 2009, in the Old Trafford match against Liverpool, Manchester United defender Nemanja Vidic brought down Steven Gerrard. Referee Alan Wiley took his time but, after thinking about what he had seen, reached for his red card. Wiley's opinion was that it was our old friend, a DOGSO.

On 22 March 2009, Liverpool were 4–0 ahead against Aston Villa at Anfield when Fernando Torres chased a ball into the Villa penalty area. Villa goalkeeper Brad Friedel brought him down so referee Martin Atkinson awarded a penalty and red-carded Freidel. Again, he thought it was a DOGSO. But Villa appealed and the panel decided it had not been a foul, so it should not have been a red card. Friedel had the suspension he was facing cancelled.

The next possible DOGSO in the Premier League was on 11 April 2009, at Wigan. Arsenal defender Kieran Gibbs grabbed Antonio Valencia's shorts and hauled him to the floor to stop him carrying the ball into the penalty area. Gibbs's face had a resigned look which seemed to say, 'I am going to get sent off here.' Yet the referee only cautioned him. Which referee? Alan Wiley. In less than a month he had changed from a man confident enough to make a big call about a DOGSO to a ref whose belief in the system had been so eroded that he settled for just a yellow card.

He was not alone. After the successful Friedel appeal, referees felt undermined.

On the specifics of the Friedel case, to my eyes the goalkeeper's actions – rushing towards Torres, then stopping and turning his body sideways to block the striker – constituted a definite foul. If an outfield player did the same in the centre circle, there would not even be a discussion if a foul were awarded.

It comes down to opinions, of course. A majority on the appeal panel were of the opinion that no foul was committed. I think 70 per cent of the population would think it was a foul. But shouldn't the opinion of the match referee be the only one that counts? If not, then how can referees have the confidence to have opinions; to make decisions? The answer to that question is that they can't. They don't.

As usual, by the way, Sky TV's 'experts' criticized Wiley for the red card he gave Vidic and for the red card he did not give Gibbs.

THE PROFESSIONALS

FIFA wanted me to succeed in 2006 because I was a professional referee and Sepp Blatter and Co were and are very much in favour of full-time, professional refs.

Yet I'd say there are plusses and minuses with professional referees.

When they were introduced in England in 2001, there was an immediate improvement in fitness, in preparation, in scientific analysis of performance and so on.

But I don't think refereeing standards have continued to improve. I don't think the referees have kicked on. In fact, there are guys who could never be given Arsenal against Manchester United, and who don't want to be given Arsenal–Manchester United. They are happy doing a few lower-profile Premier League games without being stretched.

Yet they get the same basic wage, more or less, as Howard Webb, our top official, who has to tackle all the difficult matches and is expected to put in so much more time attending UEFA conferences, talking to England's under-21 side and being a figurehead for refereeing.

Howard is on a five-year sabbatical from his career in the police to concentrate on his refereeing, and he is incontrovertible evidence that our very top officials do need to be professional and full time. But I'd like to see Howard in a European or even world elite – an international panel of referees such as exists in cricket and tennis. That elite group would referee in every international tournament and would be much better prepared when the World Cup comes around.

 **MEIN KAMPFBAHN**

THE stadium in Stuttgart where Mr Simunic and I made history has its own remarkable history.

Built in 1933, it was first named 'Adolf-Hitler-Kampfbahn'. After the Second World War, it was used by victorious US troops for baseball and called plain Kampfbahn. Next, it was called Neckarstadion (after the nearby river Neckar) and became the home of VfB Stuttgart in the Bundesliga.

By the time of the 2006 World Cup it was the Gottlieb-Daimler-Stadion, but two years later, from the start of the 2008/09 season, it became the Mercedes-Benz Arena.

Some big fixtures have been staged at the stadium. It staged West Germany's first international after the Second World War and, in 1990, the first international for the newly united Germany after the fall of the Berlin Wall. The Stuttgart stadium also hosted the final of the European Cup (now known as the Champions League) in 1959 and 1988.

SEMI-DETACHED REF

In my lifetime, only a handful of referees have been derided and then hounded by the English media in the way that I was in 2006. The very fine Swiss referee Urs Meier was very unfairly treated after disallowing a goal in Euro 2004. Another exceptional ref, Sweden's Anders Frisk, decided to retire after the treatment he received (from fans as well as the media) after sending off Chelsea's Didier Drogba in a Champions League match at Barcelona in 2005. And in 2009, Norwegian referee Tom Henning Ovrebo had to have his hotel changed so that he could not be pursued after another Chelsea game against Barcelona. Again Drogba was central to the controversy.

I am talking about the Champions League semi-final second leg at Stamford Bridge on 6 May 2009. The first leg had been goalless and so, when Michael Essien thumped in a spectacular shot to give Chelsea the lead, the London club had one foot in the Final. A second goal would probably have planted both feet there. There was thus mounting fury as the referee rejected a series of penalty appeals by Chelsea. Then Andrés Iniesta equalized for Barcelona in the last moments of the match and, when yet another penalty appeal by Chelsea proved to be in vain, it was enough to take them through to the Final by virtue of having scored an away goal. At the final whistle, Chelsea players erupted like a volcano of anger. Drogba, who had been substituted before the finish, marched back onto the pitch and confronted the referee before ranting straight into the lens of a television camera.

Now, let's establish some basics about what I think of the events of that night.

1 Do I think Chelsea should have had at least one penalty? Yes.
2 Did the referee make mistakes? Yes.
3 Was he experienced enough for such a big match? No.
4 Do I understand Chelsea's reaction? Yes.
5 Was that understandable reaction excusable? No.

To deal with number three first, I had my doubts about the appointment of the affable but unimpressive Ovrebo long before the game. When the dates of the two-legged semi-finals were announced, I calculated that the second leg at Chelsea would be the most difficult to referee. The other semi-final was between Arsenal and Manchester United, but a lot of the heat had gone out of the rivalry between those clubs. The animosity between Barcelona and Chelsea was still inflamed, however, and so the second leg – when the result of the tie would be decided – would be the one that was full of tension.

Yet, of all the referees in the four games, Ovrebo was the least experienced. That was not because he was from Norway. Despite what was said by pundits after the game, it is perfectly possible for great referees to emerge from countries where the standard of league matches is not particularly intense. Lubos Michel, who comes from Slovakia, proves that point. But Michel was in a different class to Ovrebo.

Then, before the kick-off at Stamford Bridge, I noticed that when Ovrebo's picture appeared on the giant screens in the ground, he nudged one of the assistants to draw his attention to the image. To me, that was the action of a man who was overawed by the occasion and not focusing on the job in hand.

Yet I can make out a case for him being right about each of the penalty decisions. I am not saying he *was* right, but I can see how he could argue that he was. The first appeal was when Florent Malouda appeared to be hauled down by Daniel Alves inside the box, only for the referee to signal a free-kick just outside the area. The foul definitely started outside the box and I think the ref blew too early. His mistake was that he did not give himself a moment. He did not wait for the clash between the players to finish. Had he done so, he would have seen the foul continue inside the area and should have awarded a penalty. But, he whistled too early and every referee in the world has done that more than once. Then, because he had blown for a free-kick outside the area, he was correct in Law to stick to that decision.

I'd have to say as well, though, that it is easier to give a free-kick outside the box than to be brave enough to award a penalty, especially in a Champions League semi-final. Only Ovrebo knows whether that was a consideration.

The next shout for a penalty was when Drogba was tugged back by Eric Abidal. The problem for Chelsea that time was that Drogba did not fall naturally. He went down over-theatrically – as he has a reputation for doing. With the benefit of TV replays, we could all see that it was a foul. After watching it a few times, it seems obvious to us. But at the time, without replays, I can see why the referee was not convinced that a penalty offence had occurred. And a ref cannot give a pen if he is not convinced.

To many observers, the third 'penalty' incident – an alleged handball by Gerard Pique – was the most blatant and the fourth (handball claims against Samuel Eto'o) was the least convincing. I disagree.

I think that Pique was making natural arm movements as he ran to close down Nicolas Anelka. The Chelsea player flicked the ball up and the Barcelona defender's arm continued the rhythm of previous up-and-down movements and came up to touch the ball. It looked as if it was a case of 'ball to hand' but that was irrelevant. I don't think it was intentional handball and so I don't think it was an offence.

In Eto'o's case, he turned his back as he jumped to block a shot by Michael Ballack and the ball struck his arm. I think Eto'o had deliberately raised his arm to make himself bigger. So, although it was 'ball to arm', I think raising the arm was a deliberate act by Eto'o and so it should have been a penalty.

By the end, Chelsea players, officials and supporters thought there was a conspiracy against them. But that was the cumulative result of all the penalty appeals, and you cannot add them all together to come to a conclusion. We want referees to judge every incident in a match on its merits, and so we should extend that principle to each decision a ref makes.

As a football person, I understand why Chelsea reacted as they did, but I cannot condone it. If you say that in extreme circumstances it is OK if a referee is mobbed by angry players and has to be smuggled away to a secret hotel, then you are saying something very dangerous. Every player and every manager – and every angry dad on a park touchline – thinks that the decision that has gone against him is an outrage that validates his temper tantrum. The message has to be that nothing ever justifies it.

PATH TO A NEW CAREER

At about 9.48 pm on 22 June 2006, my life could have gone in one of two directions. That was when I cautioned Josep Simunic for the second time, and if I had sent him off, then, according to Jack Taylor, I would have gone on to referee the World Cup Final. Instead, I kept my red card in my shirt pocket, left Simunic on the pitch and wrecked my credibility, my reputation and my refereeing career.

Now, years later, the pain has passed but the sense of frustration, bewilderment and annoyance are all very much still here. I am not as hard on myself as I was in the months immediately after it happened. I don't beat myself up about it any more. I don't lay awake at night thinking, 'Why?' But I haven't forgotten it and nor have members of the public, many of whom come up to me in the street and say, 'Three yellow cards!'

Perhaps that is due in part to the path I chose. After carrying on for one more season to prove that the events of Stuttgart had not broken me, I quit refereeing and embarked on a career in the media. I landed contracts with the *Daily Mail* and the BBC but my portfolio of paid commitments also includes regular after-dinner speaking. Every time I get to my feet at a dinner, I have to talk about the thing for which I am best known. That is the three yellow cards, so I have never been able to let go completely and move on.

If I had decided to return to work in sales – at which I was very successful before I became a full-time ref – then things might have been different. After a few jokes, the people I worked with and the customers with whom I was in regular contact would have got over it, I suspect. Then, perhaps, I too could have got over it more readily.

Instead, I made the choice to be in the public eye in the media and as a speaker, and so in a sense I am trading on the mistake I made. But I would not have made a Pizza Hut advert joking about the error. That is what Gareth Southgate, Stuart Pearce and Chris Waddle did after missing penalties for England at World Cups. That was their choice and I do not criticize it. But for me it would have seemed demeaning and wrong to mock my mistake so soon after it had involved hurt for the people who love me and had pitched me into a cavern of despair.

Mind you, I wasn't offered a pizza advert and I have to admit that, now, after the passage of time, I would consider making some sort of jokey ad for something involving the number three. After all, I have learned that the three yellow cards are what I am associated with, whether I like it or not.

Actually, I don't like it. It seems grossly unfair that after a career of 1,554 games, 329 Premier League matches and 100 international fixtures, the one tag that is attached to me is the one that says, 'three yellow cards'.

People ask me all the time whether I did it deliberately, to make myself marketable. Or they say, 'Are you glad it happened? It has made you famous.'

No, I most definitely did not hold myself up to ridicule in front of a worldwide television audience deliberately. No, I did not scupper my chance of refereeing the ultimate football match on purpose. No, I am not glad it happened. But I don't regret it. Life's too short. I gave refereeing my best shot and got very close to refereeing the World Cup Final. I am hugely proud of that.

I have thought about the two paths my life could have followed and, as I say in *Seeing Red*, I believe I have handled failure better than I would have handled success. I might have been unbearable had I taken that other path, the one that led to the Final in Berlin.

Instead, I was soon heading home to Tring and, as I nursed my damaged pride, I received a letter from Rob Harris. On 8 January 2000 he had refereed an FA Cup tie between Tranmere and Sunderland. Tranmere were preparing a substitution just as Harris sent off one of their players, Clint Hill. Off went Hill – and on came the substitute. The game restarted with Tranmere playing with 11 men instead of the 10 they should have following a red card. Harris was later suspended by the Premier League.

In his letter to me he said that my mistake was something which would be with me for ever, but that it would teach me some humility. It seemed to me that he was saying I needed taking down a peg or two.

But in fullness of time I came to realize that Harris's letter was heartfelt, came from a good place and was entirely accurate. I thank him for it now. It is not for me to say, but I do think Stuttgart made me more humble – certainly more humble than if I had gone on to Berlin, and far less prone to criticize others for making mistakes. That is because I know that everyone can make one.

ACKNOWLEDGMENTS

I should like to record my thanks to those who have helped my transition from referee to media man, especially Lee Clayton, the sports editor at the *Daily Mail*, who has been an enthusiastic supporter since I began writing for that newspaper.

Mick and I both thank Jonathan Taylor, Tom Whiting, Simon Gerratt, Juliette Gordon, Laura Summers and the rest of the team at HarperCollins for their keen and dedicated work on this book. We also both owe gratitude to KT Forster, our literary agent, for her patient guidance.

INDEX

character of referee 123–5, 152–6, 162, 232

cheating

  attacker causes foul against him 63–4

  'Hand of God' goal x, 57–61, 64, 65, 66, 67–8, 69–72, 74–7, 79–80, 180, 274

  honest foul 71–2

  intention to foul 62–3

  merest touch causes player to go down 63, 64–5

  player goes down without contact 62–3

  shirt pulling 64

  what constitutes? 62–4, 71–2, 75–6

  when is cheating acceptable? 62–3, 71–2, 75–6

Chelsea 18, 19, 28, 62, 104, 144, 145–6, 278, 284–7

Chesterfield 21

Chile ix, 160, 279

citing 99

Claridge, Steve 163

Clattenburg, Mark 20, 28, 29

Clichy, Gael 84

Codesal, Jose Maria 117, 122, 134

Cohen, George 2

Cole, Andy 199, 200

Cole, Joe 95

Collina, Pierluigi 152, 153–4, 162, 167, 189, 233, 241, 252, 273

Colombia 179–80, 196

common sense, referees using 113–46, 256

Community Shield, 1998 188, 189

Cooper, Keith 140

corruption 234–45, 261

Corver, Charles 90, 94–5, 102, 277

Courtney, George 22, 78–9, 227, 228

Coventry City 52

Croatia ix, 43, 195, 215, 233, 234–8, 242, 245, 250, 252, 264–76, 267

Crossley, Mark 213

Crouch, Peter 65

Cruyff, Johan 114, 148, 149, 150, 152, 156, 170, 172

Cruyff, Jordi 136

Cubillas, Teofilio 129

Cumming, George 240

Czech Republic 27, 94, 201, 244

D'Urso, Andy 69, 107, 187

Da Silva, Eduardo 105

Daily Mail 288

dangerous play 89–109, 110

Davids, Edgar 55

Davies, Barry 58–9

Dean, Mike 28, 105, 186

Delap, Rory 205

deliberate bookings, players look for 203–4

deliberately give fouls against team, referees x, 185–8 *see also* evening things up

Denial of an Obvious Goal-Scoring Opportunity (DOGSO) 211–14, 216, 217, 280, 281

Denmark 58, 73, 252

Derby County 52, 220

Deschamps, Didier 194

Dienst, Gottfried 1, 2–3, 6, 7, 10, 11, 16, 31, 277

disciplinary procedures

  additional penalties, subsequent 106–7

  citing 99

  FA 96–7